COURAGEOUS LIVING

COURAGEOUS
LIVING

DARE TO TAKE A STAND

MICHAEL CATT

EXECUTIVE PRODUCER OF
COURAGEOUS & FIREPROOF

PUBLISHING GROUP
NASHVILLE, TENNESSEE

ISBN: 978-1-4336-7121-0

Published by B&H Publishing Group,
Nashville, Tennessee

Dewey Decimal Classification: 248.642
Subject Heading: COURAGE \ MEN \
LEADERSHIP \ FAMILY LIFE

Unless otherwise noted, all Scripture quotations
are taken from the Holman Christian Standard Bible®,
Copyright © 1999, 2000, 2002, 2003, 2009 by
Holman Bible Publishers. Used by permission.

2 3 4 5 6 7 8 • 15 14 13 12 11

Dedicated to
Daniel Simmons
Pastor, Mt. Zion Baptist Church, Albany, Georgia

One of the most courageous leaders I've ever known,
my copastor, friend, ReFRESH® conference speaker,
and fellow laborer in building bridges toward racial
reconciliation in Albany, Georgia

CONTENTS

ACKNOWLEDGMENTS

This is my fourth book in less than three years. I've not had time to have writer's block. If it weren't for people helping me along the way, I wouldn't have been able to tackle such a formidable task. As I've said before, no one writes a book alone. A book is the result of people, books, and places that have influenced your thinking. It's the result of research and time alone with God. It's ultimately the result of a passion to invest in others beyond your normal sphere of influence.

When I was approached about writing *Courageous Living*, I knew I would need help. I want to thank some significant people who have helped me in this process. Jim McBride and Bill Reeves are my literary agents. They take care of the business aspect so I can focus on writing. I'm grateful they believe in me. Thomas Walters first signed me to write for B&H. His gracious guidance on this project has helped me. He challenged me to write a better book than the first draft I sent him. I hope he is not disappointed. To all the team at B&H and LifeWay, I am grateful for your belief in what God is doing at Sherwood.

To my wife Terri, who always gives me the time I need to work on these projects. She has patiently kept dinner warm so I could finish a few more paragraphs on a chapter. She reads the manuscripts and makes suggestions. She prays for me as I try to get the wording like I want it. She is my best friend.

To Debbie Toole, my administrative assistant who has served with me for twenty years. She's the gatekeeper to my office. If it weren't for Debbie, I wouldn't have the time in my schedule to get alone and write. I'm grateful she sees the big picture of what I'm trying to do.

To Stephanie Bennett, my research assistant and to my daughter Hayley, who helped me meet my deadlines. Stephanie did the initial edit and research, refining and fine tuning the material. She spends countless hours helping me get everything I need. Hayley stepped in at the last minute when Stephanie was out on maternity leave and helped me take out some of the "preachy" material and target a younger audience. With other books, I've tried to target my generation and below. With this one I needed to challenge the next generation. Hayley's insights as she read the material with a fresh eye were invaluable.

I must thank Alex and Stephen Kendrick. Not only are these guys on our staff, but they are also loyal men who model integrity and passion for their calling. I'm grateful for the powerful script and storyline of the movie *Courageous*. My prayer is that God will use the movie to inspire and challenge men to a higher level. The movie is the inspiration behind this book, and I'm grateful to share the journey with them.

To the members of Sherwood who have supported, prayed for, and encouraged me in so many ways, I am grateful. To the lay leadership of Sherwood, I'm forever indebted to them for their willingness to follow as I seek to lead. I'm especially grateful for the "Dream Team," a group of men who counsel me and help me cast vision. Last but not least, to the incredible staff God has given us at Sherwood. I couldn't ask for better men, fathers, role models, and co-laborers in the field. In all my years of ministry, these guys are the best I've ever seen.

One last word, thanks to all of you who have supported the ministry of Sherwood and Sherwood Pictures over the years. Your prayers for us and support of all we are seeking to do is a blessing to us. If God has used anything we've done—a book, a movie, or a message—we give God praise. We are nothing apart from Him. We long to "reach the world from Albany, Georgia" and see many come into the kingdom through the ministries God has entrusted to us.

Blessings,

Michael Catt
www.michaelcatt.com

WHY YOU NEED THIS BOOK AND WHY I HAD TO WRITE IT

T he story is told of a battle where the flag bearer got so far ahead of the regiment that the officer called back to headquarters and asked, "Shall we bring the flag back to the regiment?" The commanding officer said, "No, make the regiment catch up with the flag!"

Today we need men with the hearts of a warrior; men who will run to catch up with the flag Christ carries ahead of us. Men who won't turn back. We need men who stand up and take responsibility for their role as men. A recent cover of *Time* magazine (September 27, 2010) featured a picture of a young boy and his father, and the cover story was entitled, "Man Up! The Traditional Male Is an Endangered Species. It's Time to Rethink Masculinity." The article, written by Andrew Romano and Tony Dokoupil, asked the question, "What's the matter with men?" They went on to write, "For years, the media have delivered the direst of prognoses. Men are 'in decline.' Guys are getting 'stiffed.' The 'war on boys' has begun. And so on."[1] This summer *The Atlantic's* Hanna Rosin went so far as to declare that "The End of Men" is upon us.

Later in the *Time* article the authors addressed the obvious question: "If men are going off the rails, how do they get back on track?"[2] While I do not agree with all their conclusions, I do believe the issue must be addressed. Examine a few of these statements:

"When men lose, women and children lose too."

"The home is a natural place to start."

"Men have a choice: either feel inadequate or get a lot more creative."

Unfortunately the suggested image in the article appeared to be more of the feminization of men than for men to "Man Up!" Every study will tell you we are lacking in male role models today. Many of our societal problems are because of the lack of male leadership in our homes, churches, and communities. Men have walked away from family and responsibility. The impact is, according to any study, a rise in the crime rate, assault, gangs, drug and alcohol use, and imprisonment.

We need men in the church to step up. Inside the church I find that godly fathers are an endangered species. It seems the church has surrendered to the times. Rather than reminding men of their responsibilities and calling them to action, we have multiple Bible studies for ladies and softball for men. Where are the men who are resolved to invest in their kids spiritually and raise the next generation for Christ?

We need men to man up. It's time to call men to a higher level of responsibility. We need a new generation of men who don't look to the corporate office as a measure of their success. Rather, they look into the lives of their wives and children.

We desperately need men who find their significance in faith, family, and hard work. We need men who, regardless of their station in life, are stepping up to their God-given roles.

We need men to match our mountains. In these pages I explore the examples of people in the Bible who displayed great courage when playing it safe would have been easier. They challenge us to keep moving forward. They cause us to examine our priorities and deal with anything that brings fear to our hearts.

Abraham Lincoln once visited the New York Avenue Presbyterian Church to hear a sermon by the pastor, Dr. Gurley. As the War Between the States was being fought, Lincoln battled discouragement. After the message one of Lincoln's aides asked him what he thought of the sermon. Lincoln replied, "I thought it was well thought through, powerfully delivered, and very eloquent." Thus, the aide assumed Lincoln thought it was a great sermon. But Lincoln said, "No, it failed because the pastor did not ask of us something great."

I'm praying God will call you to do something great for His name and His glory. It may not make the headlines, but greatness is determined by God, not by man.

I'm encouraged by some of what I see today. I'm seeing young men and women who have been turned off by their parents' obsession with things. They are willing to be less "successful" so they can be more significant. If we can raise up an army of courageous soldiers for Christ, we can once again recapture that adventuresome faith of biblical days and win the world for Christ. It's not too late.

I'm praying that my generation will not drop the ball. There is work left to be done. I'm praying that God will raise up giants of the faith. I hope and pray this book will find its way into the hands of young people, pastors, parents, and others who will say, "By the grace of God, I will make a difference with my life. I will count the cost, pay the price, stand in the gap, and confront the culture."

I'm asking God to give the body of Christ a tenacity that seems to be strangely lacking in this hour. Caleb was an old man when he said, "Give me this mountain." Samuel was a young man when he heard from God. I'm asking God to use this book to call people from every generation and every tribe and tongue to be courageous.

WE NEED TO MAN UP!
WE NEED TO BE COURAGEOUS!
WE NEED TO DO IT NOW!

Chapter 1

THE COURAGE TO GET GOING

---

*"By faith Abraham, when he was called, obeyed
and went out to a place he was going to receive
as an inheritance. He went out, not knowing
where he was going." (Hebrews 11:8)*

*"I feel like a rich man." "You are a rich man.
You have a strong faith, children who love you,
and a wife who adores you."*

—Javier and Carmen Martinez, *Courageous*

E very journey begins with a step. I can remember watching the first landing on the moon. It was historic. I can still see it in my mind as Neil Armstrong set foot on the moon and said, "That's one small step for man, one giant leap for mankind." History is filled with stories of adventurers, men and women who dared to dream, explore, and discover. In 1953 Edmund Hillary and Tenzing Norgay became the first to conquer Mount Everest, more than twenty-five years after the first climbers attempted to top the summit. We also remember names like Orville and Wilbur Wright and Amelia Earhart, all pioneers in the world of aviation. In the church today we are seeing a new generation of missional young adults who are willing to lay aside the comforts of home to give their lives on a foreign field. I believe we are seeing a new generation of Christ followers who are risk takers for the gospel. We need more.

Unfortunately far too many live anything but an adventurous life. They seem content to be absorbed in the daily grind. They think the adventuresome life of faith is for someone else they could never become. We are among a dysfunctional society desperately in need of heroes who refuse to limit what God can do. We can't afford to buy the twenty-first century lie that our best days are behind us. I challenge you to dream big. As D. L. Moody used to say, "If God is your partner, make your plans big."

"Safety first" is not the motto of a risk taker. It may work in a factory, but it doesn't work on the field of faith. It has never been the motto of the courageous. C. S. Lewis said, "The safest road to hell is the gradual one."[1] People of courage make a way where there is no way. Instead of cowering to the pressures of this culture, Christians need to become a force for positive peer pressure. We need to break out of the box and drop the baggage. Boxes are designed for storage and shoes, not saints.

It's time to put on the shoes of faith and take an incredible journey with God. The founder of Ford Motor Company, Henry Ford, said, "I am looking for a lot of men who have an infinite capacity to not know what can't be done." God is looking for men and women who believe that with Christ nothing is impossible.

We've been lulled into settling for average so long that average seems acceptable. But I believe a desire burns within the heart of each person to make a difference, to leave a mark. Unfortunately we've been average for so long that when people are above average, we tend to think they are eccentric.

Some of the most courageous people in history were people who could have easily ended up on the shelf of mediocrity. Abraham Lincoln was a failure most of his life until he became president. Stonewall Jackson was failing as a teacher at Virginia Military Institute, yet in the crisis of battle he blossomed. D. L. Moody, an uneducated shoe salesman, ended up being one of the most famous evangelists of the nineteenth century. He also established ministries and institutions that are vibrant in the twenty-first century. The army says, "Be all that you can be." It's time for men and women to be all God saved them to be. Don't settle; soar!

My daughter Hayley remembers going to youth camps and hearing speakers tell campers they should give their lives totally to Christ without fear or hesitation. They would say, "God probably won't make you go live in a mud hut in Africa, so don't be afraid of God's will." Hayley told me, "Looking back, I was always terrified He would send me to Africa. Now I wonder why in the world I had been taught to fear that. Now I would go in a heartbeat." In 2010 she spent two weeks working in an orphanage and on a safe-water project in Uganda. As she said, "I need Africa more than Africa needs me."

An old adage says, "Nothing ventured, nothing gained." No venture, no vision, no legacy. I'm praying for God to raise up a generation who will venture out and discover the view is worth the climb. God longs to find a man or woman He can trust with a great opportunity.

The heroes of the Bible did not emerge from a cookie-cutter factory. They were all unique and distinctively different. The world is full of mimics. Fearing the opinions of others, we fall into the rut of conformity. We need mavericks. When I read the Scriptures, I see pages full of mavericks. They would not let the culture or the times define them. They refused to fit into a religious box, even if it was an acceptable box for most folks. What made them mavericks? Faith. They weren't afraid to leave a country, walk on water, confront false prophets, rebuke kings, or pray for miracles.

Warren Wiersbe noted, "Believing God means standing up and facing an impossible challenge without fear of what might happen when we obey God's will."[2] That's the attitude of the courageous. Look at the multiple examples in the Old Testament. By faith Abel offered the acceptable sacrifice. By faith Enoch walked with God. By faith Noah built an ark. By faith Abraham left his home and traveled to an unknown land. He pulled up roots, leaving everything familiar to obey the voice of God.

Let's look at this patriarch Abraham. Early in Genesis God dealt with humanity in general. When we get to Abraham, the focus shifts to one man as a model. The choices we make determine the roads we take. Choices have consequences and reveal our true character. I'm not talking about a positive attitude. I'm talking about biblical faith. We need to be identified as followers of Christ, not by the clothes we wear, the car we drive, or the house we own. Life should not be about stuff, it should be about the Savior.

I pastor a multigenerational church. I get reenergized when I see young men in their twenties and thirties making great strides in their walk of faith. They aren't willing just to be good church members. They want to make a difference with their lives. One young adult man came to me and said, "It encourages my generation to see your passion. I want you to know we hear your heart." Abraham knew life in the lap of luxury, but he was willing to walk away and be a sojourner. From luxury living to a nomadic tent is a stretch for most people.

Katie Davis is an incredible young lady who now lives in Uganda. She is in her early twenties and has adopted numerous children. She left the comfort of home at age eighteen, believing God's Word and call on her life. She believes in Christ's ability to protect, provide, and sustain. God called Katie to Africa. God called Abraham to a new land. Where is God calling you?

We each have a choice: we can be average or exceptional. We can play at church, or we can be radical for Christ. We can base our lives on the world's standards of success, or we can dig in the Bible and ask God to show us where He wants us to live and who He wants us to be.

Abraham's greater calling was to leave the land where God was largely ignored to follow the one true God. Stepping out for God always involves steps of separation. This is no time for cowards or the fainthearted. We need courage. The life of courage will see what others can't see and believe what others can't believe. Courage is a pattern and a path that will keep us going when all around us are falling and failing.

"The LORD said to Abram: 'Go out from your land, your relatives, and your father's house to the land that I will show you'" (Gen. 12:1). Abram was settled and set for life, but it was not God's plan for him to coast to the finish line. He had something more.

The book of Hebrews summarizes the courage of Abraham: "By faith Abraham, when he was called, obeyed and went out to a place he was going to receive as an inheritance. He went out, not knowing where he was going" (11:8). If Abraham had failed to obey, he would be buried in some unknown grave in present-day Iraq. No one would remember him, and no one would care.

Here was a man with no map or GPS. He didn't get a printout from MapQuest. God said, "Get out, and go on." Abraham left, not knowing where he was going. God's call is not a vacation; it's our vocation. It's time to get going. We can't sit on the sidelines any longer. We must hear God and follow hard after Him.

Leaving his home in Ur was a breakthrough in Abraham's life. Breakthroughs are turning points, pivotal moments when we are given the opportunity to believe God for something great. Abraham's obedience made him one of the most courageous men in history, as few men have cut such a broad path.

Abraham is considered the father of the faithful. Faith obeys, walks, and builds. God called Abraham, and he moved. He didn't ask for details, look for perks, or negotiate. He just got up and got going.

Our choices now have serious consequences for our future. Throughout our lives we're faced with questions like:

- Where will I go to college?
- What kind of career will bring a sense of purpose?
- Will I marry? Will we have children?

- What kind of church will I join?
- Will I choose to obey God or settle for a life of mediocrity?

My wife and I grew up in the South. After college we were trying to decide where to go to seminary. I had been offered a full scholarship to a school not very far from our home, but I didn't have a peace about it. Instead, Terri and I ended up going to a school in the North that was a twenty-two-hour drive from home. No one understood why we would move so far. All we knew was that we needed to follow God. With little money, an undependable car, no winter clothes, no jobs, and no scholarship, we set off for seminary. We have *never, not for one moment,* regretted that choice.

I can look back now and say that every significant relationship and every influence in my life spiritually has come because of that one choice. God placed people in our path who molded us and marked us. They would not let me settle for being a typical minister. They stretched me, prayed for me, and helped me. I am who I am today because of their influence.

America is a mobile society. People are constantly moving, many searching for the elusive American dream. Some move to pursue a career. Some move to escape problems. Others want a new start. Have you ever considered a move of faith?

The church I pastor is helping to plant a church in San Francisco. The lead pastor, Ben Pilgreen, has shared his vision, and others have been compelled to join him. There hasn't been a successful Southern Baptist church plant in San Francisco in nearly four decades. However, because of a calling and a vision, families are selling their homes, seeking jobs in the area, and moving away from everyone and everything they know. They are leaving nice, luxurious homes with plush backyards for small apartments in a crowded city. Why? Because of the call of God on their lives.

It takes courage for a man to lead his family to take a faith venture. Are you that kind of person? Faith, to be biblical faith, has to be courageous. Anyone can believe God once he has all the facts, but courageous faith obeys regardless of the situation.

When we began shooting the movie *Fireproof*, our oldest daughter Erin came to read for a small part. She was working full-time with Disney and knew she would only have time for a small role where she could take a few days off. As the process moved forward, the casting team began to talk about the possibility of Erin playing the role of Catherine opposite Kirk Cameron. Erin certainly wasn't expecting such a role. Taking the role would mean giving up her job, income, and insurance. Erin took that step of faith and quit her job, believing that God would provide.

During filming Erin moved back in with us. One week before shooting the final scene, Disney called and offered Erin her dream role and a contract. God blessed her obedience. She didn't play it safe, and God provided beyond her expectations. As a friend of mine says, "Jump! The net will appear!"

I don't know the name of any individual who stayed in Ur and played it safe. I do know of Abraham. Through one man a nation was birthed, the world would be blessed, and through his lineage redemption would come through Christ.

What could God do with you? Too many people spend their lives in the valley of good intentions. They start, but they never finish. Courage demands a decision. It demands we separate from the pack. It demands we lay aside secondary things, our obsession with gadgets, gimmicks, video games, fiction, and styles. Courageous people travel light.

We are to be in the world but not of it. The heroes of Hebrews 11 were polar opposites to the so-called heroes of today. In a world of celebrities and fifteen minutes of fame, we need heroes. In a culture driven by seeking stardom, we need men and women who want to be servants. In this decade of *American Idol,* we need a generation who will not worship the gods of this world and will serve the one true God.

The only way to maintain courage is through prayer. We see no altar to God in Haran or in Egypt, places of detour and delay on Abraham's journey. Isn't that true of all of us? When we detour or delay our obedience, we forget God and the promises we've made, and we start looking at circumstances.

Abraham wasn't perfect, and he made some mistakes along the way. He carried some baggage, which slowed him down. The devil doesn't have to tempt us with evil if he can get us to delay or detour for a "good" reason. To live courageously, you can't be tied down (see Luke 14:26–33). I've met countless people who have been slowed down or have stopped on the road of obedience. The courageous person faces the tests of life head-on.

Think of people you grew up with or went to school with. How many have hit bottom because they couldn't separate themselves from the crowd and public opinion? Their tombstone will read, "What could have been." Don't let that be the legacy that you leave behind.

Self-centeredness is ugly enough in the world, but it's even uglier in the life of a Christian. If you live courageously, you may lose some friends or have family members misunderstand you. The crowd thins out the higher you climb. Like Abraham, you have to decide to move on.

In some ways Abraham's life looks like a graph on the cost of living. There is the ebb and flow of life, the ups and downs, but it's always moving up. The key question is: when confronted by a test, will we obey? The self-examination question is: are you headed in the right direction or taking unnecessary detours? Work out what God is working in you.

Courageous people are willing to leave Ur (their old life) and all its enticements. They know the danger of the love of money and are not sucked in by the pride of life. Signs of Abraham's faith were the altars he built. He lived in a tent, but you find him building altars along the journey. An altar is a place of worship, commitment, and renewal. At the altar we establish a relationship with God or renew our commitments to God.

Today people want to make a name for themselves. God promised Abraham that his name would be great. He is remembered in the Faith Hall of Fame (Heb. 11). Abraham was great because his ultimate goal was to make the name of the Lord great. Abraham was a man of courage and a friend of God.

James Montgomery Boice writes, "The epithet 'friend' exalts Abraham, but it also brings the patriarch down to our level. Most of us are aware that we will never become lawgivers like Moses. We are unlikely to become generals like Joshua or kings like David. We will not be prophets, except in the sense that we are all called to be witnesses for Christ."[3]

I may never be famous, but I can be a person who hears God, believes God, and is intimate with God. I can be a person of convictions and purpose. I can leave a mark and make an impact. But I must have the courage to do it.

What drives you and motivates you? What is your purpose? In 2010 LifeWay sponsored several Fireproof My Marriage conferences. We witnessed many young couples recommitting to their marriages. I found a note from one attendee quite revealing. The man wrote that he and his wife were living separate lives. I then noticed his e-mail address and knew the problem. His e-mail address included the words *gambling* and *golf.* That said it all. Instead of loving her like Christ loves the church, his first loves were gambling and golf.

In Genesis 15 Abraham encountered God in a new and fresh way. God didn't show Abraham everything. Our responsibility is to take that initial step of faith and leave the results to God (see Gen. 15:1–8). Courage doesn't mean the absence of fear, but responding in spite of fear. This is the first time we see the words "do not be afraid" (v. 1) in the Bible. Fear is the enemy of faith. Courage will place you in a battle that fear would run from, but God is "your shield" (v. 1). That's a greater promise than an army of ten thousand at your side.

By the world's standards Abraham didn't do anything great. The largest army he ever led consisted of only 318 men. He never built fortresses or palaces, but his legacy fills the last thirty-eight chapters of the book of Genesis.

You have within you the capacity for something God sized, something so big that God is glorified through your life. To achieve that, you must walk by faith daily. Courageous faith is holy and practical. It will tune out any voice that calls you to go backwards. Too many are taking average living and mediocrity as acceptable.

Several years ago Jim McBride, our executive pastor, and I went to Green Bay to visit Kabeer Gbaja-Biamila, who was a defensive end for the Packers. He had purchased copies of *Facing the Giants* for the team and management, and he invited us up for a day to visit a practice. This was one travel decision I didn't have to pray about! Late that evening Kabeer invited us to his home. We met his family, and as we were leaving he said, "You've got to see my dog." When he moved to Green Bay, he was single and learning the Packer playbook. In the process he taught his dog several plays out of the offensive playbook. His dog knew from Kabeer's call whether to go into the tailback or slot positions or to go as a wideout. The dog knew whether to take a handoff or run a slant pattern or a down-and-out. It was amazing. As we were leaving I thought, *If a dog can learn a complicated NFL playbook, what's wrong with us? Why can't we hear the call and abandon it all? Why do we want to stay in bed when a voice is calling us to go deep?*

Throughout Scripture we are reminded that Abraham "believed the LORD and He credited it to him as righteousness" (see Gen. 15:6; Rom. 4:3, 22; Gal. 3:6; James 2:23). Paul devoted a lengthy portion of Romans to the story of Abraham, and he holds a place of significance in Hebrews 11. Is your life worth writing about?

In Genesis 17 we read, "Live in My presence and be blameless" (v. 1). God's call to courageous living is not a hundred-yard dash; it's a marathon. Walking with God requires sacrifice, commitment, and obedience. We must remember the words of Jesus when He called His followers to *leave* and follow Him (see Luke 9:57–62).

Where are you headed? Genesis 25 speaks of Abraham's legacy: "He took his last breath and died at a ripe old age, old and contented, and he was gathered to his people" (v. 8). He fulfilled his purpose and was ready to die. Nothing left to be done. He had run the race and kept the faith (2 Tim. 4:7–8). Most of us will not be great in the eyes of this world, but we can be remembered as Abraham, a man who heard the voice of God and followed, a man known as a friend of God (see James 2:23).

As a pastor, I've seen far too many who are cynical, sour, and bitter. They don't seem happy with any aspect of their lives, so they grumble and complain. I wonder what their lives would have been like if they had bought into God's plan instead of the American dream (which has become the American nightmare). Don't come to the end of your life asking, "What if . . . ?" There is a world of difference between standing at a grave and saying, "What a life!" and standing at a grave saying, "What a waste."

How will you be remembered?

Chapter 2

THE COURAGE TO CHOOSE AND REFUSE

"By faith Moses, when he had grown up, refused to be called the son of Pharaoh's daughter and chose to suffer with the people of God rather than to enjoy the short-lived pleasure of sin. For he considered the reproach because of the Messiah to be greater wealth than the treasures of Egypt, since his attention was on the reward." (Hebrews 11:24–26)

"I don't want to be a 'good enough' father. We have a few short years to influence our kids, and whatever patterns we set for them will likely be used for their kids, and the generation after that."

—Adam Mitchell, *Courageous*

John Mason writes, "The world makes room for a person of purpose. Their words and actions demonstrate that they know where they are going. . . . In your heart there is a sleeping lion called purpose. Be on a mission. Have a definite sense of direction and purpose for your life. . . . Strong convictions precede great actions."[1]

I love biographies. They give me insight into what made that person tick. God's Word is full of great biographies. These were not perfect people, but they impacted their world. They made the tough calls. You can spend your life on the wide road or the straight and narrow. There are consequences either way. One young boy's parents chose the narrow path, which ultimately led to the salvation of the Israelites.

You can't talk about Moses without talking about his parents. At a time when being a Hebrew was dangerous—and to be a Hebrew male baby was the death sentence—they rose above pressure and politics. They refused to cave in. Moses' parents knew God and believed Him for a greater purpose for their son.

Fearful parents rarely raise courageous kids. Moses' parents were from the tribe of Levi, an insignificant tribe at the time. They aren't even named at the beginning of the story, but their legacy lives to this day. The birth of Moses was a nation-changing, culture-changing birth.

Moses' father's name, Amram, means "an exalted people." His mother's name, Jochebed, means "God is honored." God's name was honored, and a nation of slaves was exalted over the mighty nation of Egypt because one couple refused to cave in to the pressures surrounding them. The birth of Moses signaled the end of four hundred years of bondage. God heard and answered. Out of slavery came a great leader. Out of obscurity came a great man.

Moses' parents lived by faith even in a difficult, if not unbearable, situation. The Bible clearly reminds us that favorable conditions do not add to faith. One of the sad testimonies of our time is the number of women who have been talked into abortions because conditions were not "favorable." Think of what might have been if abortion was still illegal. Have we lost the next great leader of this generation because we listened to and followed ungodly advice? Has fear cost us more than we can measure? We will never know.

Murdering babies was the order of the day in Egypt because population growth was a threat to Pharaoh. There are similarities here between Pharaoh's order and the order of King Herod years later to kill all the babies so he might rid the country of the supposed Messiah. Dictators often seek to eliminate the innocent.

But Amram and Jochebed sensed that their son was someone special and unique. It is important that parents give their kids courage and a sense of blessing. What you encourage and support is important. If you fear Pharaoh or the consequences of taking a stand for your faith, your children will most likely pick up clues from you. If God's Word, the church, and righteousness are not your priorities, they probably won't be priorities for your kids.

Jochebed prepared a basket for her son and placed Moses in the river, believing God would protect him. The future deliverer of Israel was delivered by Pharaoh's daughter. Jochebed then placed Moses' sister Miriam on the bank to watch. Certainly a mother wouldn't have placed her child in a position to watch her younger brother be murdered. No, she believed God would provide for her baby. Miriam was in a position to watch the Lord show up.

Moses' parents made a choice, and through their obedience God put a deliverer in the land. They feared God more than Pharaoh, and "they didn't fear the king's edict" (Heb. 11:23).

Because his parents didn't fear the king, Moses would one day stand before the king's successor without fear.

It grieves me to see how quickly some parents tear down their kids. Terri and I were in a parking lot not long ago and heard a mother screaming at her children. She threatened to leave them in the hot car or just leave them in the parking lot if they didn't do what she said.

It also saddens me to see Christian parents who do little and expect the church to do everything when it comes to spiritual nurturing. The church can't resurrect what the home puts to death. Parents today have relegated their responsibilities to schools, churches, and civic organizations, but no one can take your place as a parent.

Your kids are in a battle. If you don't fight for them, who will? Kids need parents with tenacity, tough love, and boundaries. The devil is "prowling around like a roaring lion, looking for anyone he can devour" (1 Pet. 5:8), and he wants to devour and destroy this next generation. I admire Moses' parents because they modeled a fear of God over the fear of man.

Don't be a parent who would choose fame and success for your children over faithfulness. Vance Havner said, "This adult generation lacks the backbone, grit, and courage to take an unpopular stand against Pharaoh."[2]

As a parent, do you understand your role and responsibility? You are accountable for the lives entrusted to you. Parent biblically. Are you looking to Scripture for guidance? Don't let the culture suck your kids down the sewer.

Think of it this way: you are either an eagle, a chicken, or an ostrich; and you are raising an eagle, a chicken, or an ostrich. Eagles teach their eaglets to fly. They disturb them and push them out of the nest. Eagles expect their offspring to soar. They invest in them so they will soar majestically above the crowd.

Chickens, on the other hand, teach their chicks to eat almost anything. They teach them to scratch, sit, and cackle. They have no skills to defend the henhouse against predators. Chickens never say, "You can be somebody."

An ostrich hides his head in the sand and sticks his tail up in the air. You are going to be bitten in the behind if you try to pretend the problems will go away if you just ignore them. Don't be an ostrich parent that never checks on their kids. Ostrich parents assume nothing and are surprised when something happens. They often let their kids date too early, dress immodestly, hang out with the wrong crowd, or go places unsupervised; and they ultimately refuse to set parameters altogether.

I love the story line in the movie *Courageous* that follows one of the fathers, Nathan, and his teenage daughter, Jade. Nathan makes clear to her and to an interested suitor that there are rules in his family for dating his daughter. He was a proactive dad, and we need dads like that.

A parent once came into our youth minister's office, concerned his son was watching porn on the Internet. Our youth minister asked the father where the computer was located, and he replied, "In his room." The youth minister suggested he move the computer out of his son's room and put it in a room where it was visible, like the living room. The parent responded, "That would be an invasion of his privacy." Wake up, moms and dads. You are responsible for what happens under your roof!

Let's go back to the eagle. He disturbs and ruffles the nest. He doesn't let his offspring do whatever they please. I worry about this generation of parents who seem clueless. They've taken their hands off the wheel, and their family is headed over the cliff. They buy minivans and SUVs with DVD players so their kids can watch movies on the way to and from church! We would rather entertain our kids than educate and exhort them.

Failure to be courageous in our parenting will result in a generation in bondage to the world, the flesh, and the devil. Young people today don't think for themselves. They hide behind text messages, e-mail, Twitter, and Facebook because they don't know how to have a face-to-face conversation. If they don't like the conversation, they just block you. Something has to change. If you want to raise a Moses, you can't be training your kids like a chicken or an ostrich. The failure to be a parent with courage will result in a generation of turkeys with no manners, ideals, goals, or dreams.

Like an eagle you have to demonstrate or model the behavior you expect. The eagle knows the way and shows the way. He also develops the young eaglet. He will not let his offspring lie around, eating and getting lazy. He pushes the eaglet out of his comfort zone. I want to meet Moses' parents in heaven. They raised a courageous eagle. I know he ran in fear and ended up in the desert for forty years herding sheep. But in the end Moses was God's man for the hour (Heb. 11:24–27).

Because Moses had parents who invested in him and a God who directed him, he overcame four issues that paralyze most people: Who am I (Heb. 11:24)? What choices should I make (v. 25)? What really matters (v. 26)? What is my purpose (v. 27)? Because of their example, Moses was willing to make the tough choices. The cynics of the day would have said, "What a waste. He threw away all that education, political power, and influence to live in the wilderness. He could have had greater influence if he had stayed on the inside." But God had a higher purpose for his life than being a politician in Egypt. When I read of the choices Moses made and consider the options he had, I think of the man of God described in Psalm 1:1–3.

As a young man raised in a wealthy family, William Borden made significant choices that cause us to remember him to this day. Every young man at some point has to decide, will I live for myself or for God? There's only one right answer to that question.

William Borden was faced with a difficult decision after graduating from high school in Chicago in 1904. As heir to the Borden family fortune, he received a trip around the world as a graduation present. During his travels his heart was burdened for the people hurting throughout the world, and he decided to become a missionary. As friends scoffed at this idea, Borden wrote in his Bible: "No reserves." Borden headed to Yale University and quickly stood out from the crowd, though not due to his massive wealth. A fellow student noted, "He came to college far ahead, spiritually, of any of us. He had already given his heart in full surrender to Christ and had really done it. We who were his classmates learned to lean on him and find in him a strength that was solid as a rock, just because of this settled purpose and consecration."[3]

As a college student Borden started a morning prayer group. He went after the toughest students to win to Christ, ministered to the underprivileged, got involved in social issues, and founded the Yale Hope Mission to rescue drunks off the streets. He eventually ministered to the Muslim Kansu people in China. Borden never hesitated in that calling. Though he was a millionaire, Borden kept his eyes fixed on Christ. His focus freed him to turn down many lucrative job offers after graduation. At this time he wrote two more words in his Bible: "No retreats."

Next Borden went on to Princeton Seminary and then set sail for China following the completion of his studies. He stopped in Egypt to study Arabic where he contracted spinal meningitis and died within a month at twenty-five years of age. News of Borden's untimely death quickly spread through the American media. The widow of Hudson Taylor wrote, "Borden not only gave his wealth, but himself, in a way so joyous and natural that it seemed a privilege rather than a sacrifice."[4] Prior to his death, Borden wrote two more words in his Bible: "No regrets." No reserves. No retreats. No regrets.

Borden's story is similar to that of another young man, Moses. Moses walked away from fame, fortune, power, and the pleasures of Egypt (Acts 7:22). A pagan world can never comprehend the person of conviction. It's beyond their ability to grasp, yet they are the ones wasting their lives on things not eternal.

God has a different definition of success. Moses left the palace and never looked back. He "refused" (Heb. 11:24). To refuse is to reject, deny, or totally disown. Dying to self is the most liberating decision of life. It is the defining moment that defines all other moments.

Some might say, "But Moses never saw the promised land. He did all that and didn't make it." They would be right . . . and wrong. If Moses had not taken the stand he did, he also would have never been a witness to the power and miraculous intervention of God in his generation.

Negatively, Moses refused to be called the son of Pharaoh's daughter. He rejected the sure deal. Positively, he chose to suffer affliction with the people of God and embraced the riches of a child of the King of kings. He looked at what Egypt had to offer and what God was calling him to, and he chose God. You could say he rejected the crown to take up his cross and follow daily.

We see this attitude exhibited in the believers in Thessalonica as we read how they "turned to God from idols to serve the living and true God" (1 Thess. 1:9). They forsook idols and false gods for the one true God. These new believers were barely fifty miles from Mount Olympus, where it was said the Greek gods resided. Living in the shadow of all the false gods, they saw the one true God. It's not that their false gods weren't appealing. But in the one true God, they found the false gods to be empty, meaningless, and lacking power to change their lives.

Think about the significance of Moses' choosing and refusing. Josephus tells us Moses was in line for the throne of Egypt, but he chose to identify himself with a nation of slaves. It takes courage to walk away from the crowd when "everybody is doing it." When we choose the crowd and the road of least resistance, we place ourselves on the path of compromise and carnality. We will remain ineffective in addressing and confronting the problems of this world if we continue on the path of compromise. For a Christian with courage, compromise is not an option, no matter what others say.

Not long ago I was in a discussion with a group of Christian leaders about tipping points. There are tipping points in churches, homes, marriages, morals, and ethics that act as a point of no return. Once you reach that point, it's hard to get back to what used to be. Some believe America is on the verge of a tipping point. Some feel the tipping point for our country will come by the year 2020. At that point the decay of morals, values, and the Judeo-Christian ethic, along with the rise of Islam in America, will take us to a point of no turning back.

It has been said that the only reason we are not already at that tipping point is because of the influx of Hispanics into America who are predominantly Catholic. In other words, we are approaching the cliff on the eve of destruction, and no one is applying the brakes and considering the carnage that will come. Where are the men and women of courage in our country? When God's people are silent, there is no one to confront the growing influence of false spirituality. As Adam says in the final Resolution scene in *Courageous*, "Where are you, men of courage?" If we ever needed young men to stand up, it's now.

We need courageous women as well. Courageous men and women can become courageous parents and raise courageous kids. We must ask God to raise up a generation willing to risk everything for the gospel. In 1546 Anne Askew was imprisoned and tortured in England because of her faith. She was stretched out on a rack, and her joints and bones were pulled out of socket. When she regained consciousness, she shared the love of Christ for two hours to those who were tormenting and torturing her.

The day she was led to her execution, they had to carry her to the stake in a chair because her bones were dislocated and she was unable to walk. At the last minute she was offered a pardon if she would recant. She replied, "I did not come here to deny my Lord and Master."

As young adults or as a young couple, this is no time to hesitate or be timid. We can no longer play it safe and hope that life will always be safe or easy. Hard times may be ahead for us as God's people and as a nation. We need men and women who will have the tenacity to stand.

I'm encouraged by the movement I see among young adults. They are giving themselves to Christian works and missions and taking the road less traveled. As the twentieth-century martyr Jim Elliot said, "He is no fool who gives up what he cannot keep, to gain what he cannot lose."

My challenge to this generation is simple: don't buy the lie of the prosperity gospel and Christianity lite. Give yourself to the gospel of Christ who came to seek and save the lost. Find the abundant life in the Lord, not in things. Invest in what matters for eternity. Be like Moses. See beyond the moment and make the choices that will impact a generation for Christ. Moses saw things differently. Vance Havner said, "Moses chose the imperishable, saw the invisible, and did the impossible."[5] The result was that God found a man He could trust to stand up to the most powerful dictator of the day and lead His people out of bondage.

Moses learned from his parents, and he learned in the wilderness. In that wasteland he was learning to lead. Sheep are dumb animals, and Moses was about to be the physical shepherd of Israel. He needed to learn how to lead those who desperately need a leader. He received tutelage from his father-in-law and learned about the ways of God at the burning bush. God taught him things in the desert he would have never learned in Egypt. God taught Moses the principles of life and leadership in the wilderness of obscurity, lessons he would have never learned in the lap of luxury.

Sometimes God has to slow us down to get our attention. Jim Elliot said, "I think the devil has made it his business to monopolize on three elements: noise, hurry, crowds. . . . Satan is quite aware of the power of silence."[6] When Moses left the wilderness, he was a man on a mission.

Where did the courage come from? He knew it wasn't him versus Pharaoh; it was the one true God versus all the false gods of Egypt (Num. 33:2–4). Behind Egyptian polytheism stood the forces of Satan himself. There were spiritual principalities and powers behind the earthly powers. God sent Moses to execute judgment against all the false gods of Egypt. The plagues were really confrontations against the ten gods that each plague represented. Those whom God calls will be "more than victorious" (Rom. 8:37).

Moses' parents had the courage to choose and refuse. They considered the orders of Pharaoh and refused to follow them. They chose, instead, to risk their lives and obey God, refusing to do what every other family was doing. Their decision was a defining moment. As a result of their obedience, Moses himself had the courage to choose and refuse. We need parents like Amram and Jochebed to raise spiritual giants in this land of pygmies.

How will you be remembered? Here's how Moses was remembered. "Moses was 120 years old when he died; his eyes were not weak, and his vitality had not left him. . . . No prophet has arisen again in Israel like Moses, whom the LORD knew face to face. He was unparalleled for all the signs and wonders the LORD sent him to do against the land of Egypt— to Pharaoh, to all his officials, and to all his land, and for all the mighty acts of power and terrifying deeds that Moses performed in the sight of all Israel" (Deut. 34:7, 10–12).

When you look at his life on the whole, you see a man who sized up the situation and circumstances of his day and said, "I'm going with God." Moses didn't give himself to a cause or to a movement; he gave himself to Jehovah. Martin Luther said there are only two days that matter: this day and that day. If you aren't living *this* day for Christ, you won't be ready to face Him on *that* day. What you do with God today will determine whether your life's work is wood, hay, and stubble or gold, silver, and precious stones.

What is God's will for your life? God has a plan and purpose for you. You are not here by accident (see Ps. 139; Jer. 1:5). If we learn to number our days, we will redeem the time God has given us. It's never too late to become what God made you to be. The higher you climb, the fewer choices you have. The road narrows the closer you get to the top. Decisions have to be made. As believers, the choices are between good, better, and best.

Phillips Brooks said, "A man who lives right and is right has more power in his silence than another has by his words." I challenge you to have the courage to be godly parents, to raise godly kids, and to turn this nation back to God. I challenge teenagers and young adults to be men and women God can entrust with a great opportunity. To do that we must choose and refuse. We must choose the best and reject anything less.

Chapter 3

THE COURAGE TO LEAD
ON ALL LEVELS

*"Haven't I commanded you: be strong and
courageous? Do not be afraid or discouraged, for
the LORD your God is with you wherever you go."
(Joshua 1:9)*

*"In my home, the decision has already been made.
There is no question as to who will guide my
family, because by God's grace, I will."*

—Adam Mitchell, *Courageous*

Joshua is one of the greatest generals of all time. His leadership abilities and military strategy are still studied today. Joshua was born into slavery in Egypt but eventually commanded the army of the Lord and was chosen by God to lead after Moses died. Most people begin studying Joshua's life with the book that bears his name, but there's so much more. Long before he was the leader, he had a record of obedient service and strong faith. He was willing to stand against the majority.

Joshua was undaunted by the unbelief of his peers. He was unwavering in his commitment to take the promised land. He

33

was fearless in battle, and he was a godly man at home. Joshua was the total package, a man's man.

God's call to be courageous is undeniable. How we respond to that call determines our legacy. Men and women who know they are walking in the will of God by the power of God are invincible. We need mighty men who will step up to the demands of the times because they are sure of God's call on their lives.

Joshua was a soldier and a statesman. He believed God that they could and would take the land. Joshua based his faith on the promises of God. He knew how to plan a military campaign and emerge victorious. Joshua was, in every sense of the word, filled with God, led by God, and obedient to the will of God (Josh. 1:1–9).

Some would face the crisis of the death of a leader like Moses and say, "No hope now. All is lost!" But God didn't send Joshua a suggestion. He gave him direct orders: "Be strong and courageous." With the command came a promise. God would supply all that was needed for Joshua to be a great leader.

We need strong leaders. This is no time for wimps or the weak. Our strength is not in ourselves but in the Lord. We will die just as we live. If we live as cowards, we will die as cowards. If we live courageously, we will die courageously. We want our military leaders to be courageous on the battlefield. We want our children to be courageous when facing peer pressure. We need courage to choose between good, better, and best. We need courage to stand against the status quo.

Where are the men setting that example? As I look across the pews of America's churches, I find them dominated by women and children. I find the average congregation is aging, declining, and dying. Where are the men? Why aren't they stepping up to the plate? Where are the men who are passionate for faith and family? Where are the men who are students of the Word? Where are the men of prayer?

Joshua wasn't going to waltz into the promised land. The enemy wasn't going to throw out the welcome mat and run for the tall grass. No, there would be battles. This command and the promise connected to it came at the right moment in Joshua's life. "Be strong; do not be afraid." All God's commands are God's enablement. Joshua's courage wasn't worked up; it came from God.

The truly courageous man considers God in his calculations. He doesn't forget God in his daily life, only to search for Him in a crisis. He lives with a constant awareness that "I will be with you; I will not fail you or forsake you." We are not alone in the battles, and we do not have to face the enemy in our own strength.

Fear will disable a man and an army. Fear will dismantle a country. Today, for example, we live in a world that is afraid of the consequences of standing up to radical Islam.

Dawson Trottman said, "Think! You can do a lot more than you realize." I see unrealized potential in many people today. I remember hearing John Madden say, "Potential means you haven't done it yet." Joshua realized his potential. Have you begun to realize yours? Joshua understood potential is only realized when there is preparation. Joshua made the necessary preparations to cross over and take the land that was promised (Josh. 3:5–7, 17).

Joshua's courage gave others courage. His courage gave the priests courage to lead and step into a river at flood stage.

Human reasoning would put the archers, not the priests, at the front of battle. Lloyd John Ogilvie, in his book *Lord of the Impossible*, describes the scene:

> To promise that all that water would be stopped up was quite a promise. Imagine the courage required. The Lord of the impossible had decided to make his miracle dependent on the priests getting their feet wet. Put yourself in the skin of one of those priests as, early in the morning, you shoulder the ark and move down toward that overflowing river. Now feel the strange mixture of panic and promise in your heart when the moment of decision comes. One step farther and your feet will get wet. I've always imagined that the courage needed to take that step came from the ark itself. Two parts of it would have to be daring and nerve. Inside it were the tablets on which the Ten Commandments, given to Moses on Sinai, were carved. On top was the mercy seat, recalling the forgiving, atoning love of Yahweh. Surely these priests claimed both the covenant of commandments and the mercy of the Lord as they contemplated the awesome step of faith. There was no turning back. God and the people depended on them.[1]

The river was at flood stage. Fear would have whispered, "You'll be washed away. You'll forever be remembered as the guys who lost the ark and the Ten Commandments." It takes courage to step into the water in a flood. But they moved forward with courageous faith. One day they were in the wilderness; the next day they were in the promised land.

Keep your focus on God in your calculations and contemplations. Our strength comes from standing on the promises of Christ. At some point we move from calculation and contemplation to commitment. The promise of God demanded a response. Joshua and his army had to fight as if it all depended on them. Spurgeon said, "The best and wisest thing in the world is to work as if it all depended upon you, and then trust in God, knowing that it all depends on him."[2]

Joshua was a great leader because he was a great follower. He understood duty and obedience. He knew there was an unseen hand guiding him and that God's judgment and analysis were better than his own reasoning. Who would try to defeat a mighty city just by walking around the walls? Only a man who had heard from God. After the people of God had crossed over the Jordan, Joshua went out to evaluate the situation (Josh. 5:13–15).

Joshua was a general, but he bowed before the Captain of the Lord of Hosts who was none other than a manifestation of Christ Himself. The Captain let the general know He was ready to defend His people. Joshua knew how to follow orders.

Many people are too big for God to use; they are too full of themselves. We've heard so many positive thinking, self-help sermons that we don't know how to depend on God. Lordship is a sermon you don't hear often. Yet Joshua's ability to conquer resulted from having been conquered by God.

Leaders rise to the occasion. In reality, courageous leaders like Joshua rise to the top because they've learned to bend their knees to God. There are no shortcuts to spirituality. There's no pill for courage. It is developed and defined in the quiet place.

Adrian Rogers said in a sermon, "God showed up and said to Joshua, 'I didn't come to take sides, I came to take over.'" No other leader in the Old Testament had so many battles to fight and so many foes to face. Joshua overcame them because he learned he was not in charge. God showed up not just to direct the army of Israel but to fight for and with it.

Throughout the history of His people, God has proven Himself sufficient. He never fails. He's there and He is able. Life's battles have a spiritual side. Job never knew about the conversation in heaven between God and the devil. Jesus had to inform Peter that Satan had desired to sift him. We are symbolically to dress daily in the full armor of God. We have heavenly resources available to us. Our strategies must be surrendered to the Lord's strategies. Remember, the battles belong to the Lord. It has been said that Joshua set his thinking according to the mind of God just as we set our watches according to the sun.[3]

Joshua is an example of what God can do with one person who has the courage to follow wholeheartedly. His name means "Jehovah is salvation" or "Jehovah saves." He had courage because he placed his confidence in God. D. L. Moody said, "Courage is necessary in Christian work. I have yet to find a man who is easily discouraged that amounts to anything anywhere."

Because my schedule often takes me around the country to speak in pastors' conferences and conventions, I meet hundreds of pastors every year. In spending time with these men, I've discovered many of them are filled with fear. I am increasingly burdened about those who live in fear and settle for less than the victorious life. Victory implies a battle. We are in a battle, but we shouldn't be afraid.

The Scriptures tell us "the fear of man is a snare" (Prov. 29:25). We are told to "fear not." Jesus said, "Don't be afraid." Men will follow the lead of the leaders. Sadly a church rarely rises above the level of her leaders.

Paul wrote, "For God has not given us a spirit of fearfulness, but one of power, love, and sound judgment" (2 Tim. 1:7). Leadership has nothing to do with your disposition, but everything to do with understanding your position in Christ. If you are praying for courage, do you think God will give you courage or put you in a situation where you'll have the opportunity to be courageous? You'll never know if you have courage until you are willing to be tested.

We need a new generation of courageous leaders. One day I looked around and realized the church I pastor was getting gray. We began intentionally to invest in younger men. We are seeing the blessings of that decision. Young people and young men are rising up. From middle school to midlife, I'm grateful for what I see happening in our men.

The Lord said to Joshua, "I have handed Jericho . . . over to you" (Josh. 6:2). Who among us would be willing to ask God to give us the city or the community where we live, into our hands? There's a price to pay; the price is surrender and demands obedience.

A few years ago, while traveling to Israel, my family got a huge blessing. We all flew coach for the ten-hour flight to the Holy Land, which basically means you lose all circulation in your legs. Only the grace of God and a chiropractor can straighten you out when you've been cramped in an airplane that long.

But the return trip was different. The flight was overbooked, and there were extra seats in first class. Because I travel frequently, my wife and I and our two daughters were bumped up to first class. It was a great flight. Flying first class is a different experience. The food is better. The seats are better. Everyone on the plane arrived at our destination at the same time, but we were more rested than most of our fellow passengers.

As I am writing, we are about to embark on another trip to Israel. I don't think I'll be flying first class. The only way I can, short of another miracle, is if I'm willing to pay the price. Personally, I love first class, but the upgrade is not worth an extra three or four thousand dollars. Here's the point. All believers will get to heaven, but some of us are going to get there having experienced less than God's best.

Fear of failure, fear of men, and fear of consequences will keep us crammed in a corner. It's going to take courage for you to step out of the box that the world wants to put you in and take your seat for a first-class ride. It's time to take stock of your life.

Do you long to walk in victory? Well, you aren't just going to get bumped up to first class. You are going to have to pay the price. Faithfulness in little things will open the door for bigger things. If you want to realize your full potential, you can't look for the cheap seats and the shallow end of the pool. You've got to step in, step out, and step up! That will take nothing less than courage.

Joshua was a great leader for several reasons. He faced

every crisis head-on. In his speech before Parliament on June 4, 1940, Winston Churchill said, "Whatever the cost may be, we shall fight on the beaches, we shall fight on the landing grounds, we shall fight in the fields and in the streets, we shall fight in the hills; we shall never surrender." Joshua understood the obstacles and oppositions he would face would be unique.

He didn't plot out the whole war. He took one city at a time and trusted God for a wide array of battle tactics. Joshua learned well by listening to and observing Moses. "The LORD your God is the One who goes with you to fight for you against your enemies to give you victory" (Deut. 20:4).

Just like Moses, Joshua would not compromise. The phrase "as for me" appears twenty-one times in the book of Joshua. It's a statement of courage and commitment. It's a call to renounce anything secondary and superficial. At the end of his life, Joshua was still calling the people to make solid decisions to serve the Lord.

Joshua also understood the consequences of his decisions. In chapter 24, you'll find Joshua never took credit for his success. He gave the credit and glory to God. Courageous leaders don't need applause, attention, or medals. In his farewell address Joshua reminded the people of the importance of their decisions. He knew that if you don't make the right choice, you'll suffer the consequences.

He made a famous speech at Shechem, a place where Abraham and Jacob had been. There the people recommitted themselves to the Lord after entering the land (see Josh. 8). Afterwards, Joshua took them to a place of renewal and defining moments and said, "You've got some decisions to make."

Joshua stated his family's position. He didn't ask his teenagers to vote on it. He didn't take a straw poll. I'm so weary of men always asking their kids what they think the family ought to do. My view is that if you aren't paying the bills, you don't get a vote! Joshua spoke as the head of his home (see Josh. 24:14ff).

In the movie *Courageous*, the principal men in the film make a resolution to be the spiritual leaders in their homes. Throughout the movie they display heroic acts of courage on behalf of citizens in their community, but their most courageous moment comes when they choose to stand as men and take responsibility for their own lives and the lives of their families. They commit:

> I do solemnly resolve before God to take full responsibility for myself, my wife, and my children. I will love them, protect them, and serve them and teach them the statutes of God as the spiritual leader of my home. I will be faithful to my wife, to love and honor her and be willing to lay down my life for her, as Christ did for me. I will teach my children to love God with all their hearts, minds, and strength and will train them to honor authority and live responsibly. I will confront evil, pursue justice, and love mercy and will treat others with kindness, respect, and compassion. I will work diligently to provide for the needs of my family and will speak truthfully and keep my promises. I will forgive those who have wronged me and reconcile with those I have wronged. I will walk in integrity as a man answerable to God and will seek to honor God,

obey His Word, and do His will. As for me and my house, we will serve the Lord.

Today we need men of courage. Courageous husbands. Courageous fathers. Courageous men who refuse just to "get along" by "going along." This is no time to backpedal. I think back on the days when we were having Promise Keepers meetings in our church. We had hundreds of men showing up on Saturday mornings. We took buses to the Washington Mall and made great promises. But tragically some of those Promise Keepers have broken their promises. They bought into the event, but they didn't embrace the process. They didn't apply the charge to change their ways.

The landscape is littered with the lives of those who said they were going to do something great for God and failed to do it. Where's the men's movement? I'm not talking about a pocket here and a parachurch group there. I'm talking about a global movement of men rallying to live for God and take back the land.

I refuse to preside over the death of the family and faith in silence. If this culture is going to collapse, I'm at least going to stand and speak. Not long ago I shared this message with the members of Sherwood and said, "I stand as a pastor and father, challenging you to follow God though none go with you. You and I can't worship the one true God and worship something or someone else" (see Josh. 24:14). What we worship is what we spend our time thinking about. That's why the battle in the New Testament is in the mind. We must renew our minds and think on these things because God has called us to think differently than the world thinks. But until right stands up and looks like right, then wrong doesn't take it into consideration."

There are no do-overs in this. You only get one chance to cross the Jordan, conquer Jericho, take the land, and be a godly man. Choose this day whom you will serve. That was the cry of Joshua's heart in his last sermon. What will your farewell speech sound like? Will it be, "I'm sorry I wasn't . . . I didn't . . . I should have . . . I wish I had . . ." Or will you be able to say, "I bowed my knees to God and surrendered to Him years ago. I've never regretted that decision. I led my family to serve God." By the way, you've been writing your farewell speech with every day of your life. Will you edit it today because it's not the kind of speech you want to leave? Or can you say, "As for me and my house, we will serve the Lord"?

This is not a dress rehearsal. The battles are real. The demands are great. The opportunity to make a difference is immeasurable. It all begins with you and your house. Samuel Rutherford said, "After I've given Him all I am, I must still say, 'Lord Jesus, come and conquer me!'" The Moravian missionaries started a revival that lasted more than one hundred years. They never looked back. They moved forward in courageous faith. Their motto was, "Our Lamb has conquered! Let us follow Him." Let the same be true of us.

Chapter 4

THE COURAGE TO BE A HUMBLE HERO

"The LORD turned to him and said, 'Go in the strength you have and deliver Israel from the power of Midian. Am I not sending you?'"
(Judges 6:14)

"I am very grateful to have a job here, but I cannot do what you have asked of me. Because it is wrong. I cannot dishonor my God or my family by lying on the report."

—Javier Martinez, *Courageous*

We are in a leadership vacuum. You hear it in the media. The question is often asked, "Where are the national leaders for political parties?" It seems leaders today are nothing more than the bland leading the bland.

Several years ago the *Los Angeles Times* carried an editorial entitled, "Whatever Happened to the Public Heroes of Yesterday?" The journalist wrote, "We live in an age of spiritually timid and lackluster men, for whom the very concept of bold leadership is anathema."[1]

I have to agree wholeheartedly. I see it in education, business, government, and politics. Unfortunately I also see it among God's people. We need to find leaders. We need heroes. If we are going to see significant change in our lifetime, we must stop hiding in fear. We have an incredible opportunity to make an impact if we don't lose our way. Who knows, a hero may be hiding inside of you.

Most people we call heroes never view themselves that way. They didn't get up one morning and decide, "Today I will be a hero." But their stories fill the pages of history.

Most of us remember the heroes of September 11. Some tried to take over the cockpit of an airplane, uttering the unforgettable words, "Let's roll!" That phrase still reminds us of common people turned heroes who will be remembered in history books. Firemen and police officers ran into the World Trade Center to face a dangerous task, reminding us that public servants across the country who risk their lives on a daily basis are some of our greatest unsung heroes. Hundreds of them died that day, doing their jobs, trying to save lives, and hoping to make a difference.

With the movie *Courageous,* our desire is to call men to be heroes, to be men of honor for their wives and children. Honor begins at home. We want dads to see that good is not enough. We want to raise a generation that looks to their dads with admiration, not indifference or scorn.

The heroes in my life are men and women from all walks of life; you've never heard of most of them. My dad was a hero, but probably fewer than five hundred people ever knew his name. He was a hero in his high school as one of the best athletes to ever play football or basketball, and some of his records still stand sixty years later. He served in World War II with the atomic bomb squadron. I have pictures of him standing by the *Enola Gay* when Colonel Paul Tibbets brought her home after dropping the first atomic bomb.

When my daughter Hayley was in high school, she wrote a paper about my dad. We contacted Colonel Tibbets to see if he remembered my dad. I can still remember his response: "He was an American hero." The weight of his statement stunned me. My dad never saw himself as a hero. He was just doing his job and serving his country, handpicked by Colonel Tibbets to be part of a highly secretive group of men.

Paul wrote to the Corinthians,

> Brothers, consider your calling: Not many are wise from a human perspective, not many powerful, not many of noble birth. Instead, God has chosen what is foolish in the world to shame the wise, and God has chosen what is weak in the world to shame the strong. God has chosen what is insignificant and despised in the world—what is viewed as nothing—to bring to nothing what is viewed as something, so that no one can boast in His presence. (1 Cor. 1:26–29)

God raises up people to achieve His purposes. They would not choose themselves for such a task, but God sees something in them and calls them out. Most of us would not consider ourselves to be heroes, but God has chosen us, handpicked us to be His servants. God has a way of taking nobodies and making them into somebodies through the power of Jesus Christ.

During the Welsh Revival, Seth Joshua prayed, "God, would you raise up a man among us, from the coal mines or behind the plow, so it doesn't pander to our intelligence." One of the great lessons believers have to learn is our strengths are no help to God and our weaknesses are not a hindrance. John Blanchard says, "God thinks most of the man who thinks of himself least."

Gideon was a young man who was totally convinced he was a nobody. Today he's considered a hero. God is not looking for talent or personality; He's looking for someone He can trust with great responsibilities. He looks for those who will give Him glory. Humility is not thinking poorly of oneself, but rather it means not thinking of oneself at all.

The book of Judges is depressing. The fact that such a book would follow the story of Joshua is a sad testimony to a generation that decided defeat and defiance was better than victory and obedience. A generation arose that did not know God, just two generations removed from the days of Joshua.

They compromised, fell into sin, and were ultimately bound in servitude. While in bondage they prayed for a deliverer but never appointed one. God always chose the one who would lead, and Gideon is one of the judges God raised up in a time of crisis.

Gary Inrig, in his book *Hearts of Iron Feet of Clay*, writes, "One of the great truths of Scripture is that when God looks at us, He does not see us for what we are, but for what we can become, as He works in our lives. Other people look at us and see our flaws and failings. God looks at us and sees our possibilities, through His transforming presence."[2] I often tell people who are down on themselves, "God wants for you what you would want for yourself if you had enough faith and sense to want it."

You should find great encouragement in the story of Gideon. God is in the business of making nobodies into somebodies. Don't let others tell you what you can be; let God tell you. When I first started in the ministry, the pastor of my home church told me I should never expect to do anything "great" because I was more of a "behind-the-scenes supporter" than a leader. He encouraged me to "settle." Maybe I was a late bloomer, but I knew I wanted to make a difference with my life.

When my dad died, we were gathered at the funeral home for visitation. My Aunt Hazel was there. I wish you could have met Aunt Hazel (not really). I don't ever remember her smiling; she had the spiritual gift of discouragement. Aunt Hazel walked up to two of the ladies on our staff and asked them who all the people were at the funeral. They told her many were members of Sherwood. She seemed stunned and asked, "How many members are in that church?" When they replied, "Three thousand," she quickly responded, "Hum! I never thought that boy would amount to anything." So much for family support!

I'll bet you have an Aunt Hazel. There's someone who always tells you what you can't do, what you could never do. Don't listen to her. Your Aunt Hazel never did anything with her life, so don't let her put you in the same box.

The Scriptures provide accounts of men and women who seemed insignificant on the surface, but they were important enough to include in God's Word. Men like Shamgar, who is mentioned only twice in the book of Judges. "After Ehud,

Shamgar son of Anath became judge. He delivered Israel by striking down 600 Philistines with an oxgoad" (3:31). We know little about this man, but we do know he used an agricultural instrument and saved Israel. God took note of him.

No one initially tagged Gideon as a great leader. He was probably the last person people expected to be called to greatness by God. The full account of his encounter with God is told in Judges 6, but take note of the interchange.

> The Angel of the LORD came, and He sat under the oak that was in Ophrah, which belonged to Joash, the Abiezrite. His son Gideon was threshing wheat in the wine vat in order to hide it from the Midianites. Then the Angel of the LORD appeared to him and said: "The LORD is with you, mighty warrior."
>
> Gideon said to Him, "Please Sir, if the LORD is with us, why has all this happened? And where are all His wonders that our fathers told us about? They said, 'Hasn't the LORD brought us out of Egypt?' But now the LORD has abandoned us and handed us over to Midian."
>
> The LORD turned to him and said, "Go in the strength you have and deliver Israel from the power of Midian. Am I not sending you?"
>
> He said to Him, "Please, Lord, how can I deliver Israel? Look, my family is the weakest in Manasseh, and I am the youngest in my father's house."
>
> "But I will be with you," the LORD said to him. "You will strike Midian down as if it were one man." (Judg. 6:11–16)

For seven years the Midianites and Amalekites and other nomadic tribes humiliated God's people. They constantly raided, raped, and pillaged the nation. The once great people under Joshua were now nothing more than a two-bit, second-rate people, being beaten like a drum by the surrounding tribes and nations. Why? Sin and unfaithfulness to God.

Gideon didn't run up and volunteer to lead an army. He was hiding, a coward who would, over the course of time, become courageous. At first we are struck by Gideon's hesitancy and fear. Yet when the Angel of the Lord appeared, He called this coward a "valiant warrior." The expression refers to brave soldiers who marched into the teeth of the enemy. It's a word for a hero, a person who shows remarkable courage. God wasn't being sarcastic; rather He was looking through the long lens of eternity. God could see Gideon and what he would become. It was a heavenly evaluation. God saw something in Gideon that Gideon didn't see in himself.

Thus Gideon responded with words of unbelief. Over and over he uttered words like *if, why, where, but,* and *how.* In response to all his questions and concerns, God said, "Go in the strength you have and deliver Israel from the power of Midian. Am I not sending you?" God didn't tell Gideon to go in his own power. He told him to go in the power of God, for God was with him and would be with him.

Maybe fear weakened Gideon. Fear of fighting. Fear of dying. Fear of the unknown. Regardless, courage certainly didn't define him at this point in his life. The list of phobias in this world is endless. There are the more common phobias like arachnophobia, the fear of spiders, or pteromerhanophobia, the fear of flying, and then the outright strange phobias like halitophobia, the fear of bad breath, or megalophobia, the fear of oversized objects, or even phobophobia, the fear of having a phobia!

Fearful people are often indecisive, and this seemed to be the case with Gideon. But God has a way of taking indecision and turning it into acts of heroism. It begins with an encounter with God. God didn't just see who Gideon was at the moment, but He also saw who he could be wholly yielded and surrendered. In fact, I find some sanctified humor in God finding a man who was hiding and giving him an army that had to be dwindled down to a few hundred. God wanted Gideon to move from fear to faith, from cowardice to courage.

Today we lack courage because we foolishly try to prop up our self-image and sense of worth with a little pop psychology and a dash of religion. Self-help books may work on the surface, but they don't change the heart or character of a man. God wasn't trying to prop Gideon up; He was reminding him that provision had already been made to meet the demands.

God's power transforms us into something we could never be on our own, and His Word is His promise. For example:

What then are we to say about these things? If God is for us, who is against us? (Rom. 8:31)

I am able to do all things through Him who strengthens me. (Phil. 4:13)

For God has not given us a spirit of fearfulness, but one of power, love, and sound judgment. (2 Tim. 1:7)

Warren Wiersbe writes, "Like Gideon, we are prone to argue with God and try to convince Him that His statement of our potential is greatly exaggerated. Moses took that approach when God called him (Exod. 3–4), and so did young Jeremiah (Jer. 1); but both of them finally gave in and surrendered to the Lord's will. It's a good thing they did, because that was the making of them."[3]

God is committed to His plan for your life, no matter your weaknesses. We do not need self-help, self-confidence, or a pat on the back. We need to appropriate our confidence in the greatness of our God. One evidence of Gideon's growing God-confidence was his destruction of the altars of Baal on his father's property (Judg. 6:25–32). Courage at home. In their place he built an altar to Jehovah. This was a serious test that could have brought the wrath of Gideon's family, but courage demands that choices be made.

There can be no peaceful coexistence or detente with the devil. If I lack courage at home, I'll lack courage in the battle. Gary Inrig reminds us, "Until Gideon put things right in his own backyard, God would not and could not use him to deliver his people."[4] Gideon's obedience and courage led to his father's repentance. When they discovered the destroyed altars, the men in the town wanted to kill Gideon. But, probably to Gideon's surprise, his father defended him (Judg. 6:29–32).

Joash saw his son's courage and the ineptness of Baal to defend himself, so he gave his son a new name, Jerubbaal, meaning "contender with Baal" or "anti-Baalite." Gideon was a walking reminder of the ineptness of the false gods and the power of the one true God.

The two altars in the story of Gideon represent two powerful truths. The first altar is for Jehovah who reigns. The second is a reminder that Baal is finished. Until we have the courage to throw our false gods overboard, we'll never live courageous lives. Something will always be dragging us down.

In 2000 our family visited England and Scotland. On that trip we met an incredible man named Colin Peckham who took us on a tour of Edinburgh. As we walked along, he pointed out the grave of John Knox. We also toured the Knox home and walked down to Holyrood Palace. As Colin told the story of John Knox and his boldness, his eyes brightened, and his voice resounded with power, recalling a day when a single man stood for what was right. Because of John Knox, Scotland experienced the Reformation.

Colin recounted the familiar story of Knox being a prisoner on a slave ship because he would not submit to the established Catholic Church and because he preached repentance, even to Mary Queen of Scots. One day someone brought him a wooden image of the Virgin Mary and demanded he kiss it. Knox refused, grabbed the statue, and threw it overboard. Then he shouted, "Let her save herself! She is light enough; let her learn to swim." That one act of courage propelled Knox to the forefront of the Reformation.

Courage is not courage until it is put to the test. Hudson Taylor said, "All of God's great men have been weak men who did great things for God because they reckoned on His being with them; they counted on His faithfulness."[5] Because of his stand, the Spirit of the Lord came upon Gideon. An army was assembled numbering thirty-two thousand, but on paper they were no match for the enemy army numbering 135,000.

The odds were impossible. No one would have bet on Gideon except God Himself. In fact, God was so sure of the outcome that He had Gideon cut the army down to three hundred.

I've visited the site of this historic victory and the springs several times. It's incredible to stand there and think of what happened on that day when God showed up and showed out. The 135,000 were camped to the North. Between the two armies were a valley and the spring of Harod. At the spring God began the process of dissolving the great army and reminded Gideon that power and courage and victory are from the Lord alone. Gideon had too many soldiers, and God knew they would take credit for the victory. Twenty-two thousand left in fear, but God wasn't finished. There was another test.

> Then the LORD said to Gideon, "There are still too many people. Take them down to the water, and I will test them for you there. If I say to you, 'This one can go with you,' he can go. But if I say about anyone, 'This one cannot go with you,' he cannot go." So he brought the people down to the water, and the LORD said to Gideon, "Separate everyone who laps water with his tongue like a dog. Do the same with everyone who kneels to drink." The number of those who lapped with their hands to their mouths was 300 men, and all the rest of the people knelt to drink water. The LORD said to Gideon, "I will deliver you with the 300 men who lapped and hand the Midianites over to you. But everyone else is to go home." So Gideon sent all the Israelites to their tents but kept the 300, who took

the people's provisions and their trumpets. The camp of Midian was below him in the valley. (Judg. 7:4–8)

Gideon was looking for fighters while God was looking for faith. The men chosen were the ones who left one hand free and two eyes open. Some of us are too big for God to use. We are proud of our strengths, gifts, talents, personality, education, and training. But God is looking for desperation, brokenness, humility, faith, and obedience, and He shares His glory with no one.

God had instructed His people regarding courage in Deuteronomy 20: "When you go out to war against your enemies and see horses, chariots, and an army larger than yours, do not be afraid of them, for the LORD your God, who brought you out of the land of Egypt, is with you. . . . Do not be cowardly. Do not be afraid, alarmed, or terrified because of them. For the LORD your God is the One who goes with you to fight for you against your enemies to give you victory" (vv. 1, 3–4).

If fear is contagious, courage is also contagious. Fear focuses on the obstacles; courage focuses on the opportunity. Fear sees with eyes of flesh; courage sees with eyes of faith. This test of drinking from the spring was a test of courage. Gideon was instructed to watch the men as they drank, and only three hundred kept their eyes on the enemy. Oliver Cromwell once likened his New Model Army to Gideon's. He said, "Three hundred good men and true with fear of God in them is better than 10,000 swept together by chance conscription or picked up for a shilling a head in the public house."

When Gideon and his men perhaps should have been afraid, the Midianites were actually afraid. In the end it was

God versus 135,000, and the 135,000 didn't have a chance. Gideon and his band of brothers were merely instruments in the hands of God.

This incredible account reminds us that God is not looking for great people; He's looking for available people who will follow Him. Victory comes by faith. God is not limited to your way of reasoning. It only takes one person full of the Spirit to make a difference. One writer said, "Not only because they fight more bravely, or that they obey orders more promptly, but because God is pleased to vindicate such a company, no matter how small, because its only hope for victory in the conflict lies with him. He will not have us boasting that we have saved ourselves by our own strength. But his delight is to have his people celebrating victories won against all human odds because he has been their deliverer."

Regarding faith, Ron Dunn writes,

We can divide faith into three categories. First, there is the kind of faith that says, "God can." We believe God can do anything. Nothing is too hard for Him . . . but this is not victorious faith of which the Bible speaks. It is passive and accomplishes nothing. Then there is faith that says, "God will." This is better, but still short of the biblical ideal. . . . The faith described in Hebrews 11:1 believes beyond God can and God will. It believes God has. This kind of faith declares it already done. Instead of waiting for God to create the provision, it steps into the provision already available. . . . Anyone can believe he has something after he receives it. That's walking by sight, not by faith.

Biblical faith is believing you have something before you have it. You believe you have it because God says you have it and not because you see it in your hand.[6]

In light of those words, read carefully these promises to Gideon:

The LORD is with you, mighty warrior. (Judg. 6:12)

The LORD turned to him and said, "Go in the strength you have and deliver Israel from the power of Midian. Am I not sending you?" (Judg. 6:14)

"But I will be with you," the LORD said to him. "You will strike Midian down as if it were one man." (Judg. 6:16)

The LORD said to Gideon, "I will deliver you with the 300 men who lapped and hand the Midianites over to you. But everyone else is to go home." (Judg. 7:7)

That night the LORD said to him, "Get up and go into the camp, for I have given it into your hand." (Judg. 7:9)

Are you facing overwhelming odds? Does it seem you are outnumbered? Do you feel inferior or helpless or inconsequential? Be strong. Take courage. Let the Spirit of God through the Word of God empower you and embolden you.

Chapter 5

THE COURAGE TO FACE AN UNCERTAIN FUTURE

"Do not persuade me to leave you or go back and not follow you. For wherever you go, I will go, and wherever you live, I will live; your people will be my people, and your God will be my God. Where you die, I will die, and there I will be buried. Yahweh punish me, and do so severely, if anything but death separates you and me." (Ruth 1:16–17)

"People who go through this, and learn to trust in the Lord, find a comfort and an intimacy with God that most people never experience. . . . God doesn't promise us an explanation, but He does promise to walk with us through our pain."

—Pastor Rogers, *Courageous*

I love the women of Courageous. The wives, Victoria Mitchell (Renee Jewell), Carmen Martinez (Angelita Nelson), and Kayla Hayes (Eleanor Brown), represent women who are facing various crises of faith. In each family, there are situations and circumstances that test them and tempt them to fear.

Fear can cripple you or destroy you. In tough times we are often paralyzed by fear of the unknown. Because fear is such a powerful force, we've often dealt with it in our movies from Sherwood Pictures. In *Flywheel* we dealt with the fear of losing all of one's possessions and the respect of a son. In *Facing the Giants*, we dealt with the fear of failure, infertility, and the loss of a job. In *Fireproof* we addressed the fear of a failed marriage. And in *Courageous* we address issues of fear that bombard parents on multiple levels.

Fear is believing a lie, listening to negative voices, and not taking God at His Word. As my dear friend Manley Beasley put it, faith is "believing that it's so when it's not so, so that it can be so because God said it's so." Faith is fear that has said its prayers. In the story of Ruth, we find a situation where fear could have destroyed two women and, in reality, the course of a nation. While Ruth is an incredible story of courage, in the opening verses we find a woman who is facing life with the cloud of death hovering over her. It's a story of famine, pain, and uncertainty.

Whether it is the death of a child, a marriage, or a dream, many are called to confront an uncertain future. One of my favorite people on the planet is Kasey Ewing, the middle daughter of my longtime friends, Charles and Penny Lowery. She and her husband, Brad, currently serve at First Baptist Church of Bossier City, Louisiana. They are difference makers. But their lives have been filled with pain that most of us pray we never experience. Like Ruth, their lives have been marked by death and an uncertain future, but they've maintained their courage. Kasey shares their story:

In August of 2001, on a bright Sunday afternoon, our lives changed forever. Our family had just driven home from Sunday lunch. Brad had to return to church, and he let the boys and me out of the car. I took the boys into the house, but our youngest didn't follow; he ran back to be with his daddy and ran behind the car.

The car hit him. Chaos erupted, neighbors came running out, an ambulance was called, family arrived at the scene. Brad rode in the ambulance with Jake screaming for his daddy, moving in and out of consciousness. That day Jacob "Jake" Gunner Ewing met his heavenly Father face-to-face.

Dr. Fred Lowery (Kasey's uncle), speaking at the funeral, said, "Jake was running to meet his earthly father and was welcomed by the arms of his heavenly Father." Reflecting back after Jake died, a dangerous shift occurred in me. I pretended well. I was surrounded by many people I loved and wouldn't quit loving, but as much as I could control, I wouldn't allow new possible hurts in. I began to see people as possible new hurts so I shut myself off mentally.

Somewhere deep down I really thought that if I just stopped feeling, I might stop hurting. I resurrected a wall, or maybe even a fortress, surrounding my heart.

I was never one who threw fits with God. I cried but rarely had public outbursts. I hurt but rarely admitted it. I felt I had to be strong, had to prove I was doing OK. I felt the weight of my response to Jake's death as a personal responsibility to the rest of the world. I quietly assumed that I had to be strong and stoic in fear

that those around me might not think God is good.
I picked up a burden I was not able to bear along with
my grief.

Less than two years after Jake's death I was preg-
nant with Jackson, another little boy. I was scared to
love him yet couldn't help myself. Jackson is the kind
of boy who demands you love him with everything
you have. Jackson was just what I needed to force me
to feel. The choice wasn't up to me. He demanded and
received my full heart. He was just too wonderful to
withhold my affection.

God is faithfully widening the holes in my wall,
slowly letting light in. Shielding oneself is not the
answer. Exposure is.

The story of Ruth is one of the most inspiring short stories
ever written. It unfolds before us like widening holes in a
wall. It takes place during the time of the judges and begins
with three funerals and a famine. The time of the judges
was a depressing time. Now the depression became personal.
Darkness surrounded these women on every side. The deaths
of their husbands left Naomi and her daughters-in-law, Orpah
and Ruth, shrouded in grief. Death has a way of making the
unknown seem unbearable. The emotional ambushes are real.
Whether it is the death of a parent, child, or spouse, the pain
is real.

The story of Ruth encourages us to be courageous. It
should be a ray of hope in any difficult season. It tells us that
God rules and overrules. It reminds us that God knows what
is going on in the most seemingly insignificant of lives.

If you have ever walked through the death of someone you love, you will have no problem putting yourself in the story of Ruth. This story of bereavement turns into a story of blessing. Neither Naomi nor Ruth knew it at the time. Ruth was a Moabite married to an Israelite from Judah. Scripture gives no indication of how spiritually minded her husband had been. But once he passed away, what would she do? Bad news was persistently pounding on her door. Death, darkness, hurt, fear, and grief were her daily diet. But every place has a purpose in the economy of God.

To make matters worse, her mother-in-law and sister-in-law were grieving as well. I'm sure people offered them trite comforts like, "You'll get over it." But you don't. Or, "Time heals all wounds." But it doesn't. "You'll always have your memories." But what you really want is flesh and blood to hug and hold.

Naomi decided to return to Bethlehem, the small town she and her husband Elimelech had left because of a famine. Ruth was determined to go with her. That took courage. This was not an easy decision. They had no way of making money. Two women traveling alone could have been assaulted and left for dead on a dark street or in a dark valley. Remember, Bethlehem was the location of the gang rape (Judg. 19). And because Ruth was a despised Moabite, no Jew would have felt obligated to help her.

Ironically, *Bethlehem* means "the house of bread." Naomi and her family had left their home because there was no bread. Now, as Naomi and Ruth returned to God's promised land, the time of harvest was beginning (see 1:22). You may be going through a dry time right now. Your life may be overwhelmed by drought and famine. Maybe you are in a drought financially or spiritually, but take courage. Ruth reminds us there is hope in the darkest of times.

Orpah decided to take the easy path, staying in Moab. Ruth chose the harder course, having no idea how she would be received when she arrived in Bethlehem (see Ruth 1:16–22). The selfless response of Ruth to Naomi is the hinge on which the door of this story swings. Ruth's willingness to follow would result in a blessing for Ruth and Naomi and ultimately for Israel and all who believe. Ruth displayed greater faith than the people of Israel during this time.

God said to His people, "Wherever you go, My presence will go with you." Ruth said to Naomi, "Where you go, I will go, and where you stay, I will stay." God said, "I will be your God and you will be My people." Ruth said, "Your people will be my people and your God my God." Ruth exhibited great faith in a time of great testing. Her words represented a covenant, which invoked a curse on her if she failed to keep her promise. This response also carried legal implications. What might seem on the surface like two insignificant women and one insignificant decision became one of the most pivotal moments of redemption history.

Ruth embraced the God of Abraham, Isaac, and Jacob. Given the opportunity to go back to idolatry and tribal gods, she chose the God of Israel. Her decision to accompany Naomi was a public profession of her bold declaration, "Your God will be my God." Ruth made a deliberate decision. She stated her convictions, and nothing would persuade her to do anything differently.

Naomi was no encourager of faith for Ruth. As the women

returned to Bethlehem, she complained of her lot in life. She no longer wanted to be called *Naomi*, which means "pleasant," but *Mara*, which means "bitter." Naomi felt God had treated her unfairly, and she pointed at Him with an accusatory finger. "'Do not call me Naomi. Call me Mara,' she answered, 'for the Almighty has made me very bitter. I went away full, but the LORD has brought me back empty. Why do you call me Naomi, since the LORD has pronounced judgment on me, and the Almighty has afflicted me?'" (1:20–21). Naomi had built walls around her life. She had been hurt, and she wasn't trying to hide it.

It's easy to assume this attitude, especially in our culture of entitlement. Or when you feel you haven't gotten your slice of the American dream. "The world owes me." "God owes me." "I deserve better." "I should have more." When life slaps you with the unexpected, you can choose to respond like Naomi or Ruth.

While Naomi referred to God as the "Lord," His covenant-keeping name, she was accusing Him of not keeping His word. She felt God had mismanaged her life. But Ruth rose above Naomi and didn't allow bitterness to poison her. She exhibited courage in her affirmations that are still quoted to this day.

Warren Wiersbe writes, "She was living in a Jewish family that evidenced very little faith in the God they professed to serve. Naomi let her circumstances make her bitter. Ruth let them make her better. Ruth's attitude brought a blessing that cannot be measured."[1]

Ruth acted with courage, although no blessings had been promised that she could cling to. She had no husband, no children, and no way of earning a living. She would be a stranger in a foreign land.

I've always admired the story of a young single woman named Corrie ten Boom. She was, without question, a woman of courage whose family paid a price for their faith as they hid Jews in their home in Holland to help them escape Nazi persecution. On February 28, 1944, someone turned their names in to the Gestapo. The house was raided and the family imprisoned.

Corrie's father Casper was told he could be put to death for saving Jews. He said, "It would be an honor to give my life for God's chosen people." He died ten days after his arrest at age eighty-four. Corrie and her sister Betsie were detained in three different prisons before finally being sent to the concentration camp at Ravensbruck near Berlin. In the end, four members of the ten Boom family gave their lives to save others.

When Corrie was miraculously released at the end of 1944, she returned to Holland and devoted her life to this thought: There is no pain so deep that God's love cannot reach it. She started a worldwide ministry and traveled to more than sixty countries during the next thirty-three years.

Corrie died on her ninety-first birthday, April 15, 1983. According to Jewish tradition, only those persons specially blessed by God are granted the privilege of dying on the same date of their birth. Corrie ten Boom was a woman of faith and courage. She overcame unbearable circumstances and lived with persecution and death.

As Ruth's story—and God's sovereign provision—unfolded, she had to find a way to make a living. While Ruth just "happened" to glean in the fields, God used a man named Boaz as a picture of grace: "She happened to be in the portion of land belonging to Boaz" (2:3).

Boaz allowed Ruth to glean in his field. He even made sure she had water and plenty of provisions because he had heard of her love for Naomi. He ordered his reapers to glean the sheaves and deliberately drop handfuls of barley so Ruth would have more food.

She said to him, "Why have I found favor in your sight that you should take notice of me, since I am a foreigner?" Boaz replied to her, "All that you have done for your mother-in-law after the death of your husband has been fully reported to me, and how you left your father and your mother and the land of your birth, and came to a people that you did not previously know. May the Lord reward your work, and your wages be full from the Lord, the God of Israel, under whose wings you have come to seek refuge" (2:10–12).

When Ruth asked why she had found *favor,* the word means "the unmerited grace and mercy of God toward His own." Ruth recognized Boaz was a godly man, and, in turn, Boaz recognized Ruth's faith in God. God used this man to begin to turn the tide in Ruth's and Naomi's lives. Hope was on the horizon as Boaz took an interest in Ruth and watched over her.

Ultimately Boaz would become the Moabite's *kinsman-redeemer.* The term is used thirteen times in this story. The *Dictionary of Biblical Imagery* notes:

> The kinsman-redeemer was a near blood-relative and always male. This near-kinsman (or one of them, if many) had a duty to protect his weaker relatives. He had to redeem property belonging to relatives when they had to sell land or goods (Lev 25:23–25) and

even their persons when they had sold themselves into slavery (Lev 25:47–55). For example, Jeremiah bought land belonging to his cousin at Anathoth because he was the kinsman-redeemer (Jer 32). In the case of Ruth, it was important that the nearer relative give up his right/duty in favor of Boaz (Ruth 4:6). The kinsman-redeemer was also duty bound to come to the defense or aid of a relative in either a legal or an actual struggle. This adds meaning to Job's foresight of the Redeemer on his side (Job 19:25) and underlies the Lord taking up the role in defense of his people when he saw no one else coming to their aid (Is 59:15b–20). That God would act as such a redeemer proved his family connection with those he was to save.[2]

Ruth even reminded Boaz that he was a kinsman-redeemer. Despite the fact that Boaz was older and Ruth was a younger woman, she chose Boaz. By redeeming Ruth, Boaz made her his wife. There was another kinsman-redeemer, but he wasn't interested in fulfilling his obligations. Boaz was willing to step in and fulfill the role.

In chapter 1, Ruth didn't know Boaz existed. In chapter 2, he was merely a benefactor but became a protector. In chapter 3, she initiated a relationship with him. In chapter 4, Boaz secured her future by going to the city gate and taking the necessary steps to fulfill his role. If there was ever a "Cinderella meets the prince" story in Scripture, this is it.

It all began when Naomi suggested a custom that tends to make readers uncomfortable, but that was acceptable among God's people at the time. There is no suggestion that anything immoral happened. Ruth was simply calling Boaz to take up his God-given responsibility. Warren Wiersbe writes, "Life is sometimes filled with 'rude awakenings.' Some of these awakenings are pleasant, and some are unpleasant. Adam woke up and discovered that God had created a wife for him. Jacob woke up and discovered that he was married to the wrong wife! Boaz awoke at midnight and discovered a woman was sleeping at his feet."[3]

In Genesis 38 and Deuteronomy 25, we learn that it was imperative for a man's family name to be preserved. If a man died without an heir, steps were to be taken to ensure he had one to carry on his name and inherit his property. It was required by God that the widow of a dead man be married to one of her husband's relatives. Neither Naomi nor Ruth had an heir, so Ruth appealed to Boaz to be her kinsmen-redeemer. She exchanged her widow's garments and put on fresh clothes. It was time to break with the past. First she came under the protective wings of God, and now she was coming under the protective wings of her redeemer, Boaz (Ruth 3:9–13).

Ruth refused to spend the rest of her life wallowing in grief and self-pity. Rather, she put feet to her prayers and works to her faith. That night as she laid at Boaz's feet, she was putting herself in a position of submission and surrender, first and foremost to the will of God for her life. Don't read this part of the story through twenty-first-century eyes. Read it in the context of the times and the covenant. Ruth is a model of a godly, bold woman of faith. In effect, she approached Boaz and said, "Thanks for praying for me, but let's face it, you are my kinsman-redeemer. It is up to you to keep the covenant. Boaz, you are the answer to my prayers and to yours." Faith demands courage. It takes risks and acts according to God's Word.

As a pastor, I listen to women who are begging for their husbands to step up and be spiritual leaders. They long for the man of the house to be a godly man. They want their husbands to take the wheel. They want their children to see their daddy as a spiritual leader. They long for a husband who loves them *and leads his home.*

The romance of Martin Luther and his wife Katherine is a true love story. He called her, "Kitty, my rib." She had been a nun but left the convent and lived in Wittenberg. Luther actually tried to help her find a husband, but she refused. After two years Katherine informed Dr. Luther that if he were to ask her to be his wife, she would not say no.

On June 13, 1525, Martin and Katherine were married. He was forty-five, and she was twenty-five. It was an incredible marriage and broke down the concept that men in ministry were to be unmarried and celibate. In many ways Katherine was an industrious woman, starting a variety of ventures to feed the family, as Luther would not take royalties for his books. Katherine also cared for six children and, at times, eleven nieces and nephews as well as constant guests. Because of her, Luther was free to impact the world.

I admire strong women. My wife is a quiet but strong woman. I don't believe the Bible calls women to be doormats. Submission doesn't mean being a second-class citizen. Throughout history, strong women have impacted this world for Christ. Many had the courage to stand out in a time when women were, in fact, treated as second-class citizens. If courage begins at home, it must also be present in the wives and mothers and daughters, as well as the husbands and fathers and sons.

Several years ago I met a most amazing woman. Terri and I were in New Mexico speaking at a conference, and we met an incredible lady named Rose. She serves as one of Southern Baptists' North American missionaries. As she shared her story, we began to weep. Rose is more than a survivor; she is an overcomer. She blossoms in the desert. She reflects the abundance of Christ on a Navajo reservation. Her friends and family call her "Lady Moses."

Rose is a Navajo Indian whose name means "taking my time to be born." Her parents were alcoholics. Her mother died when she was thirteen years old. On March 4, 1964, she and her eight-year-old sister set out to find the home of an aunt and uncle, having no idea a blizzard was approaching. The girls were dropped off at a bus stop and began walking. Along the road the blizzard hit full force. The girls were not dressed for such extreme weather. Rose's sister died during the night. The next day Rose and her deceased sister were found in a four-foot snowbank by their uncle's dogs. Rose said, "It was really freezing. My whole body was frozen. When I was cold and asleep, I heard a voice in my ear. I saw a board shape in a picture frame with something written on it. It said, 'Believe in the Lord Jesus Christ and thou shalt be saved' (see Acts 16:31). I had never seen that verse before. I had never read a Bible."

She was in a coma for three days, not knowing her sister was dead. She was hospitalized for two-and-a-half months because of severe frostbite in her feet. One Friday, Rose overheard a doctor saying they were going to amputate her foot. Up until that point, she had a cover over her legs and had not looked at them. When she looked at her left foot, it was the size of a football. As Rose lay back on her pillow, she prayed in her native language, "God, you have saved my life from the cold, cold weather. I accept You. I want to follow You no matter what it takes. I will walk with You. I really believe. Please heal my foot." By Sunday when the doctor checked her foot, it was healed.

After she got out of the hospital, she lived with her aunt and uncle, but they did not support her embracing the "white man's religion." Eventually she was evicted from her aunt and uncle's home, but the pastor of the church, a Southern Baptist missionary, took her in.

Rose has never married. She says, "My ministry is to the Navajo." She is still on the reservation, pointing her people toward Christ. She teaches a weekly class to Navajo women and teenagers because she wants them to be able to read the Bible in their native language. Rose spends many of her days going door-to-door to share the love of Christ. Because of her faithful witness, Rose's father came to saving faith in Christ, and many of her family members now know the Lord. She continues to pass her faith along by recording the New Testament in Navajo.[4]

Life can come out of death. Ruth and Boaz married and had a son, Obed. He was the father of Jesse, the father of David. The sleepy little town of Bethlehem became famous. The "house of bread" would ultimately become the birthplace of the Bread of life. Ruth became part of the genealogy of Jesus Christ (Matt. 1:5).

We can face an uncertain future or great loss or unexpected tragedy and grief with courage, knowing our heavenly Father cares for us and brings life out of death.

Chapter 6

LOOKING FOR MILLENNIALS WITH COURAGE

"Let no one despise your youth; instead, you should be an example to the believers in speech, in conduct, in love, in faith, in purity."
(1 Timothy 4:12)

"What I want for you is that you seek the Lord and that you trust Him even if means you are standing alone. . . . You got me?"
—Adam Mitchell to his teenage son Dylan, *Courageous*

Before becoming a pastor, I was a youth minister for fifteen years. I was blessed to come along when the emphasis on discipleship was beginning. I was never cut out to be a "cookies and Kool-Aid" youth minister. I wasn't interested in babysitting students because I believed (and still believe) students needed to be challenged.

I wanted my students to be courageous on their school campuses. Today dozens of men and women who came through our ministry are serving the Lord. I regularly get a text, e-mail, or tweet from one of them telling me what God is doing in their lives.

We often hear that Jesus' disciples could have been teenagers. If Jesus entrusted His message to teenagers, why do we try to entertain them? He believed they could handle truth and a worldwide ministry, but we aren't sure they can behave for an hour. What has changed? I believe the answer can be summarized in one word: expectations. We don't expect much, and they don't disappoint us.

My expectations are high for this generation. We can't change the culture and reach the nations if we don't expect our young people to step up to the challenge. Sammy Tippitt shared the following story with me:

Before the collapse of Communism and the fall of the Berlin Wall, Germany was a divided nation. West Germans lived in freedom, while East Germans lived under the strict ideology of Communism. Berlin was one of the most unique cities in the world, divided by the Berlin Wall. East German soldiers stood in towers on the east side of the wall, poised to shoot and kill fellow countrymen who tried to escape to the West.

Christians were especially targeted with persecution. Huge cathedrals were virtually empty due to pressure from the Communists. A young person had to make a decision at the age of fourteen whether to be a part of the Free German Youth (Communist youth organization) or a member of the church. If they chose the church, they were limited in their educational opportunities. Consequently, young people left the church en masse.

In that context I (Sammy) ministered to the youth of East Germany, even though it was illegal for them to meet with me. I once met secretly with a group of young people in the basement of an old castle. I encouraged them to follow Jesus fully. At the close of the Bible study, one young person with tears in her eyes told me, "I am a new believer. But I have sin in my life, and I don't know what to do."

She began weeping, confessing, and repenting of sin and asked God to enable her to serve Him completely. She cried to God, "I am willing to serve You and follow You." Then she added a phrase, "No matter what it costs." The rest of the young people went to their knees, crying out to God with the same surrendered heart and concluded with the same phrase, "No matter what it costs."

Two friends and I had gone to East Germany to minister to those young people. But the truth is that they ministered to us. They taught us the meaning of true courage. They faced the loss of education, the possibility of poverty, and a future filled with difficulties. Yet they prayed, "No matter what the cost." They drew courage from the cross.

What did it produce? A spirit of revival gripped the youth of East Germany. Within two years of that meeting, I again spoke to the youth of their city, Dresden. This time more than 2,000 filled the service. Several years later the wall came down. I feel certain that the courage of those East German youth played a role in freedom coming to the nation. It was the power of their prayer, "No matter what the cost."

I'm asking God to raise up young men and women in this land who will pray for God to use them no matter what the cost. Thom and Jess Rainer in their book *The Millennials* make the point that for many Millennials, Christianity is a family heirloom rather than a faith commitment. Their research discovered that only 13 percent of Millennials mention religion, faith, or spirituality as an important part of life. Only 65 percent of Millennials were willing to call themselves Christian in even the broadest sense of the word.

Millennials' most common belief about life after death is "no one really knows" (34 percent). Thom and Jess Rainer's research analysis reveals that 67 percent of Millennials say they rarely or never "read the Bible, Torah, Koran, or other sacred writings." In light of this, should we be surprised that our culture is decaying? Only 46 percent agree strongly that God is a real being, not just a concept. Four in ten agree strongly or somewhat that Satan is not a real being but just a symbol of evil. Half of Millennials believe that when Jesus walked this earth He sinned like other people, and only half agree that Jesus is the only way to heaven.[1]

All this research illustrates the need for a sweeping movement of God among young people today. We need Him to move on the hearts of this generation like He did in the 1940s during the days of Youth for Christ. We need another Jesus Movement. We need another college revival like the one at Asbury College. These movements changed lives, impacted a generation, and shook the church. Out of these movements came some of today's great Christian leaders. Where are the young college students willing to change their generation?

The term *teenager* is a relatively new one. In their book *Do Hard Things*, Alex and Brett Harris note that the first documented use of the word *teenager* occurred in an issue of *Reader's Digest* in 1941, less than seventy-five years ago.[2] It's an age that marketers look at, study, and target. Before the mid-twentieth century teenagers were, in a sense, nonexistent. Kids went to school, worked the farm, or learned a trade. There was little time for extracurricular activities. In reality the clothing was not that different from what adults wore. How times have changed.

The period of time between childhood and maturity is difficult. It's tough being a teenager. But we must raise up a courageous generation who will rise up to take their place and embrace their responsibilities. We can turn the tide.

Because of the decay of the home and the influence of media and entertainment, students are languishing in a cesspool of uncertainty. They don't know who they are or why they are here. They don't understand absolutes. If they have a belief system, they may not be able to define it or even articulate it. And they are biblically illiterate. It will take a radical change to begin thinking biblically.

The graying church is leading us into a cemetery. Everywhere I go, I challenge pastors and churches to reach the next generation. I have challenged my church to be the church where all generations are wanted. A place that an alienated kid can call home. A hotbed for raising up the next generation of preachers and missionaries. Among the laity, I'm asking God to give us people of all professions who are first and foremost disciples, skillfully disguised as bankers, sales clerks, waitresses, teachers, and physicians. I'm praying this generation will see their jobs as what they do to pay the bills but their calling to be game changers for the gospel.

I am grateful for the adults who served in the children's and youth ministries while my girls were growing up. I'm grateful for leaders like Jay Strack, founder and president of Student Leadership University, who believed we needed to start investing in students as leaders. By the grace of God both our girls have chosen to serve the Lord. Erin uses her gifts in the world of entertainment, and Hayley is a gifted writer and photographer with a heart for missions and orphans.

Terri and I have enjoyed watching our children grow in the nurture and admonition of the Lord. We never expected our girls to be good just because I was a pastor. We expected them to have a healthy fear of God. By His grace we never experienced the ugly years of rebellion and resentment.

We taught our girls that rebellion was never against our opinions but against God's authority. As a parent of a preschooler, child, or teen, you've been given clear instructions to steward wisely the lives entrusted to you. This cannot be passed off to the school or the church. Give them the encouragement they need to stand for things that matter.

While I know there are no guarantees against having a prodigal, there is no need for parents to set themselves up for failure. If we are going to see a generation of courageous kids, it's got to start with parents who instill a "no matter what the cost" mentality into their children. Following Christ should not be multiple choice in your home. If it is, you're setting yourself up for heartaches and headaches.

In the movie *Courageous*, Adam, one of the fathers, has a struggle with his son Dylan, a typical fifteen-year-old. Dylan feels his dad loves his younger sister more than him. Dylan needs to respect his dad, and Adam needs to learn to communicate with his son. It's a genuine picture that even in a Christian family, life is not perfect, and it takes work to build character in our kids. I would never say there aren't issues and challenges, but the teenage years don't have to be lethal and gut-wrenching. The more parents are involved (without meddling) in the lives of their kids, the better chance we have of raising a courageous generation.

I love to think of Daniel when I think of a young person who made a difference. He's a great example for Millennials to follow. Nebuchadnezzar wanted some of the young Israelite men in his court. Rather than killing everyone, he asked his right-hand man to find some young men who had their act together. The king ordered him to look for the men who stood head and shoulders above their peers, young men with potential that he could put through a crash course in Chaldean culture (see Dan. 1:1–4).

Many scholars believe these young men were between the ages of thirteen and sixteen. They were brought in to be brainwashed in the godless culture of Babylon. Everything they believed would be challenged, and they would face intense peer pressure. But note the words of Scripture regarding Daniel: "Daniel determined that he would not defile himself" (1:8). Daniel made a covenant in his heart that he would not cave in to the culture.

Among the thousands of young men brought into the land, two stand out: Ezekiel and Daniel. Both were godly young men. Daniel displayed the one quality necessary for a person to soar spiritually: courage. He dared to stand up for what he believed. His courage wasn't just for a moment; it was a way of life.

We need a generation to rise up with the mind-set of Daniel, Amos, Ezekiel, and John the Baptist. We need a generation that fears God more than men. Daniel is a great example to follow, regardless of your stage in life.

Daniel was tested at the king's table in Babylon (Dan. 1:8ff). As a young man with great faith, his heart and mind were in tune with Jehovah. Although he was just a teenager when snatched out of his home, separated from his parents, and thrown into a strange environment, he stood for what he believed. Even when faced with enormous pressure and potentially deadly consequences, he never wavered. The early test defined him.

Daniel's resolve was the launching pad for all the decisions made throughout the rest of his life. He knew what he believed and why he believed. He learned to live according to God's Word. As someone once said about the Scriptures, "Know it in the head, stow it in the heart, show it in the life, sow it in the world."

Eating the king's meat and drinking from his wine cellar would have been a violation of Jewish law. Daniel knew to partake would have been viewed as a sign of compromise and even approval. Therefore Daniel purposed and resolved not to partake. Imagine passing up food fit for kings in order to honor the unseen God. Daniel was convinced and convicted that it was the right thing to do. He stood his ground, and his decision was vindicated (see Dan. 1:12–19). Even the king had to admit that Daniel was head and shoulders above all others.

It's never right to do wrong; it's always right to do right. Just because everyone else is doing it, doesn't mean you should. Most individuals would have caved in and compromised. They would have argued to eat and live another day, saying, "What's the harm in a few ribs? Nobody back home will ever know. Our parents aren't here to check on us." That line of reasoning has led more than one college freshman into the pigpen of a distant land.

In *Courageous* we meet a young man searching for love and acceptance who turns to gang activity and violence in his quest for a sense of family and belonging. The gang leader tells him, "We're family now," after he is initiated into the group by means of a harsh beating. Teenagers today are looking for a place to fit in, a place to be accepted and loved. Unfortunately most do not have the courage or the encouragement to stand against societal pressures and make wise decisions in the face of evil.

Daniel lived a purposeful life. He didn't make rash decisions. His faith was not hit or miss. His appetite for the things of God gave him no appetite for worldly things. Daniel refrained from revelry, although the Babylonians were known for their physical excesses. Before Paul wrote, "Do not be conformed to this age" (Rom. 12:2), Daniel lived it.

Yet Daniel maintained a gracious spirit. Being courageous doesn't mean you can be unkind. The fruit of the Spirit is not eliminated by boldness. Daniel simply lived what he believed with the perfect balance of boldness and gentleness.

Spiritual warfare is a battle of the mind. Daniel faced a trial of the mind when the king demanded that the wise men interpret his dream. If they failed, they would die. They tried to bargain for time with the king but got nowhere (see Dan. 2:10–11). Then the king ordered the wise men to be killed. When Daniel learned of the situation, he asked for an audience with the king and told Nebuchadnezzar he would interpret his dream. Then Daniel gathered his three friends for a prayer meeting.

Talk about courage. They were looking for Daniel to kill him, and he asked for an appointment with the king. It took courage to pass this test. Daniel was wise enough to call in his prayer partners. God gave Daniel a vision of what had happened in the dream. What he delivered to the king was not good news, but it was the truth. While the magicians lost their nerve, Daniel faced the situation head on. He didn't waver, even while delivering news of judgment and doom and the demise of the Babylonian Empire.

Daniel's honesty and truthfulness turned the heart of the king. "Then King Nebuchadnezzar fell down, paid homage to Daniel, and gave orders to present an offering and incense to him" (Dan. 2:46–48). If you want to be courageous, get alone with God and ask Him to make you bold. God will use you publicly if you allow Him to tutor you privately.

In the third trial we find Daniel in the lions' den. His faith led him there. Daniel served the Lord faithfully, but faithful service does not make one immune from tests. King Darius was on the verge of making Daniel the prime minister of the nation. Out of jealousy and envy, his peers set a trap for him.

They couldn't question Daniel's integrity or character, so they devised a plan of attack (see Dan. 6:4–10).

Daniel didn't compartmentalize his faith; it defined who he was at the core of his being. His faith didn't stem from convenience but conviction. While Daniel's enemies played on the king's ego, Daniel did what he had always done. He went home, threw open his windows, and prayed toward Jerusalem. He never forgot his roots, and he never compromised his character.

The person of courage is willing to face the consequences of his decisions. We may stand alone, but we are never alone. It never entered Daniel's mind to compromise. Not one time did he consider being politically correct. Although he was in the lions' den, the only person who lost sleep that night was the king. Daniel slept like a baby while the king tossed and turned wondering what happened to the man of God.

Daniel was a young man who became an old man and lived a consistent life. He remains one of the most powerful examples and influential leaders in all of human history. While living in a pagan culture, here was a young man who proved that you can stand for God.

One of the great regrets of my life is that I spent my high school years playing games and playing church instead of living for God. I wasted those years trying to please people who have never cared a thing about me. Most of the folks you strive to impress as a teen won't ever talk to you again after graduation. The reality is that I worried about what they thought of me, and they weren't even thinking of me! They were too absorbed in thinking about themselves.

This generation is living in a postmodern world. The day of the Judeo-Christian ethic is largely over in America. We are a chameleon culture, blending in so we don't stand out. In this environment we need millennials who will have the courage to define the culture, not let the culture define them.

Some folks think if they are going to live for God, they have to be nerds or outcasts. They respond with a legalistic approach to life rather than with an understanding of balance and order. Daniel stood head and shoulders above his peers. But he wasn't weird; he was wise.

Courageous millennials need godly wisdom. Proverbs 1:7 reminds us, "The fear of the LORD is the beginning of knowledge; fools despise wisdom and discipline." If a millennial wants to be a game changer, he will have to learn to listen and be wise. John Calvin said, "This is our wisdom, to be learners to the end."[3] Wisdom is not just acquiring information or filling in the blanks in a notebook. When people possess true wisdom, they don't have to apologize for their actions. My mentor Vance Havner used to tell me, "If you lack knowledge, go to school. If you lack wisdom, get on your knees!"[4]

Studies show that in grades seven through twelve, the average teenager listens to eleven thousand hours of music, yet they are in school only seven thousand hours. If a teenager was in church every time the doors opened, it wouldn't even touch the hours of influence from the world. Jim Elliot, a missionary who was martyred in Ecuador, wrote out Psalm 119:37 in his diary: "Turn my eyes from looking at what is worthless; give me life in Your ways." Following the entry he wrote of "the decentralizing effect (of television) on the mind and affections.

It quickens me in ways not of God, defeating the purpose of prayer to be quickened in ways Divine."

As a youth minister I had two rules: (1) When in doubt, don't. (2) Be where you are supposed to be, when you are supposed to be there, doing what you are supposed to be doing. Those two pretty much cover every life situation. Your choices determine your legacy. Daniel chose wisely.

Billy Graham said, "Courage is contagious. When a brave man takes a stand, the spines of others are often stiffened."[5] Here's my bottom line as a pastor and father: I want the next generation to take back the land we've squandered in my generation. We need a generation to rise up who will stand for Jesus no matter the cost. *The New Rebellion Handbook* defines *courage* as a "willingness to go the distance when the vision has faded, when you're weary, when no one is there to cheer you on. Courage is an enduring commitment to be your true self when no one is looking and you're facing intimidation. . . . Courage has many faces. Is yours one of them?"[6]

I pray that many Millennials will be the new face of courage in our land. In years past we've seen God do incredible things through young men and women who were willing to be used by Him. I'm praying, "Lord, do it again."

There have been seasons in the past when God raised up a young generation to become spiritual giants. My friend Warren Wiersbe tells the story of one such movement, Youth for Christ.

Youth for Christ was a ministry of faith, bathed in prayer, that resulted in sacrifice and service. The compelling vision was to reach lost teens and get them into churches where they could grow. Like Abraham, we went out not sure where we were going, but the Lord directed us. Bob Cook used to remind us, "If you can explain what is going on, God didn't do it."

The official motto was, "Geared to the times, anchored to the Rock," and this meant we felt free to use any legitimate means to spread the gospel: music, books, quizzes, skits, singspirations, rallies, holiday conferences, etc. It was remarkable the way pastors, missionaries, businessmen, senior adults, and teens rallied together, prayed together, and worked together. Local YFC ministries sprang up seemingly spontaneously in the United States and Great Britain and then almost worldwide. *YFC Magazine* began early in the movement, now known as *Campus Life*.

Apart from the Lord's blessing, why did it succeed so amazingly? Partly because after World War II, teenagers finally became a recognized part of society. They were spending lots of money and creating lots of problems. Before YFC, very few local churches had youth pastors; today almost every church has a youth ministry. YFC also sent many teens to Christian colleges, and many new schools sprouted up.

There was a wonderful unity among the workers. I don't recall any denominational squabbles. Our statement of faith was evangelical, so we were united in Christ and the gospel. Had we focused on denominational distinctive, we would have grieved the Lord and probably wrecked the ministry. Ted Engstrom used to say, "YFC is grounded in the Word, founded on the Word, and bounded by the Word."

The Christian teens themselves were at the heart of the harvest. They prayed, took their Bibles to school, witnessed, invited their friends to the YFC clubs and rallies, and maintained a good reputation at school and church. Many of them are today ministering as pastors, teachers, missionaries, and faithful Christians in many areas of life.

We were severely criticized by some famous Christian leaders, but the Lord took care of that. Our policy was to love them all, pray for them, and avoid public debates that could only multiply the problems. Time has vindicated YFC. I wish I had a list of the "famous" people (so called) who came to Christ through YFC. Ravi Zacharias comes to mind. Billy Graham was a vice president of YFC for many years and used his influence to strengthen and expand it.

Lord, raise up a new generation that will be used to turn this nation back to You.

Chapter 7

THE COURAGE TO MAKE UP YOUR MIND

---

*"Then Elijah approached all the people and said,
'How long will you hesitate between two opinions?
If Yahweh is God, follow Him. But if Baal,
follow him.'" (1 Kings 18:21)*

*"I struggled with who I was my whole childhood. I
almost got in a gang myself. If fathers did
what they're supposed to do, half the junk we
face on the street wouldn't exist."*

—Nathan Hayes, *Courageous*

I magine you're nineteen years old, critically wounded, and dying in the jungles of Vietnam. Your infantry unit is outnumbered eight to one, and the enemy fire is so intense that your infantry commander has ordered the medevac helicopters to stop coming in.

As you lie on the ground, you know in your heart you aren't getting out. Your family is twelve thousand miles away, and you'll never see them again. Suddenly you hear the faint sound of an approaching helicopter. You look up and see it's an unarmed Huey without any medevac markings on it. The pilot is not part of the medevac unit, so this isn't in his job description, but he flies into the fire anyway. He lands in the middle of the battle and loads you on board to rescue you out of the gunfire.

The pilot's name was Ed Freeman, and he kept coming back, a total of thirteen times. He rescued nearly thirty wounded warriors who would have otherwise died on the battlefield. One brave man can make a difference. Freeman later received the Medal of Honor for his outstanding heroism.

Recently Matt Chandler wrote on his blog, "There are lots of neat Christian guys but very few godly men." We need godly men. In 1 Kings 18 we see the difference one godly man can make: "Elijah is here!" (v. 8). When Elijah showed up, everything changed. No one could be neutral as to the presence of Elijah. He was either a troublemaker or a problem solver, depending on which side you were on.

When Elijah showed up, the false prophets and idolaters knew a confrontation was coming. I imagine the sound of his voice, rumbling across the mountains like the sound of thunder. His impact was always substantial. He could stop the rain and call down fire. No one could be passive about Elijah.

Where is the man of God that the world takes notice of today? When Elijah prayed for the rain to stop, it was a physical reminder that the nation was going through a spiritual drought and needed to return to God. Rain is a symbol of God's blessings in revival. He prayed, and the skies withheld showers of blessings for three years.

Where are the men with backbone? Where are those who can stand against public opinion and speak for God? Elijah was a man who didn't hesitate to call people to make up their minds about God. It's time for every husband and father to call his family to a decision. The days demand a faith that cannot be compartmentalized. The average church member might like a sermon on Elijah, but they would change churches if Elijah was called to be their pastor.

God is on the lookout for men and women wholly surrendered to Him. The answer is either yes or no; there is no in-between (see 1 Kings 18:21). Jesus said, "You are either for Me or against Me."

We need a man of God to rise to the occasion today. It's time to give away the man purse and skinny jeans (Does anyone look good in those?) and man up. Men need to step up and stand up. The tide will turn when we decide enough is enough.

In the midterm elections of 2010, the Tea Party got a great deal of attention. Whether you agree with them or not, they got attention because they had made up their minds about Washington politics: "Enough is enough. We want our country back!" You may not agree with them, but I'm looking for some men who will stand up to a carnal, casual attitude toward the things of God and say, "Enough is enough!"

Not long ago I was preaching a series called "Raising the Next Generation for Christ." I want young couples to know how important it is to disciple their children. A best-selling author of more than thirty-five books was visiting our services that day. As I sat down after the service, I said to him, "I am so weary of the complacency of the average American church." His immediate response was, "I'm so refreshed that you are weary of it."

Today on Mount Carmel there's a statue of Elijah with sword in hand. Even the statue seems to shout, "Elijah is here!" As you stand on that mountain, you can see the Valley of Armageddon below. One day in that valley the King of kings will show up to confront all His enemies, and on that day all will know: "Jesus is here!"

Elijah is found on the pages of the New Testament more than any other Old Testament prophet, appearing more than twenty-five times. He represented the prophets on the Mount of Transfiguration. John the Baptist reminded people of Elijah. And when Jesus asked, "Who do men say that I am?" some answered that He might be Elijah. He is an example of a man of prayer in the book of James. Elijah is known, not for any books he wrote, but for the deeds he did. He was a man of action and a man of prayer. To be effective in your work for God and for your family, you have to be a person of prayer.

How do we turn the tide? We challenge men to lead out no matter the odds. People want leadership. Vance Havner said, "Elijah was no superman; but he could pray. He prayed down fire and water."[1] We need both today. We need the fire of the Spirit and the showers of revival. God is looking for such a man. He is looking for a man who will say, "Here am I, send me." "For the eyes of Yahweh, roam throughout the earth to show Himself strong for those whose hearts are completely His" (2 Chron. 16:9).

We need an Elijah because in our society the godless are ruling, and too many don't care. The faith that once cost people their lives doesn't even motivate us enough to be faithful to the local church. At the rate we are going, it's not terrorists we should fear; it's God removing His protective hand from this nation. Where are the Elijahs of God?

We need a person of courage to stand and call us to wake up (see Rom. 13:11–12; 1 Cor. 15:34; Eph. 5:11–14). Why do we need to wake up? Most of what I see and hear encourages me to have a sense of entitlement, not sacrifice. Where is the one who, "calls on Your name, striving to take hold of You. For You have hidden Your face from us and made us melt because of our iniquity" (Isa. 64:7)?

We've listened to politicians, and they've failed us. We've listened to experts in the media, but they seem to know less than we do. We've listened to those who give us sugar coated pop psychology, yet it doesn't work. What we have in this media age is a pooling of ignorance. What we need is a leader who will stand up and call us to desperate prayer.

Elijah was a man's man. He didn't blend in with the Christianity-lite crowd. I'm personally embarrassed by many men in churches who lack backbone. We have incredible men from all generations in our church. The one constant I hear from men who want to make a difference is: "Tell it straight. Don't lighten up. Call us to commitment. We don't need you to soft sell what God demands of us."

Men are more committed to hunting, fishing, and sports than to Christ. They would never think of turning down tickets to a ball game or an invitation to a hunting trip, but they'll roll over and turn the alarm off if it's raining on Sunday morning. I don't care how old you are, you aren't a man until you take responsibility and live in accountability.

Let me ask you a brutally honest question: Which is more important to you—hunting, fishing, off-roading, following your favorite team, or time in God's Word? If you spent as much time on your hobbies as you do on your walk with God, how good would you be at your hobbies? If you spent as much time on your walk with God as you do on your hobbies, what kind of man would you be?

How will we know if God has given us an Elijah? He will do what Elijah did. He will hide himself in prayer and then show himself and call for a decision. He will demand that we make up our minds. "If Yahweh is God, follow Him. But if Baal, follow him" (1 Kings 18:21).

D. L. Moody heard someone say that God was waiting to show the world what He could do through one wholly surrendered man, and Moody responded, "By the grace of God, I'll be that man." Who could be that man today? It could be you as a dad. It could be you as a young person. Whoever it is, we need you now. God is walking the aisles today, stopping at every row to see if there is a man whose heart is set on Him.

God sent Elijah on the scene to judge and confront. J. Sidlow Baxter noted, "When wickedness develops into extraordinary proportions, God meets it with extraordinary measures." Elijah was God's man to take the initiative away from the godless king and queen, Ahab and Jezebel. Elijah showed up and threw down the gauntlet. He boldly declared, "It's not going to rain until I'm ready for it to rain." Imagine being a weatherman in Israel during those days. Every day the forecast was the same: hot with a zero percent chance of rain. At least they knew how to dress!

Three years later the land was living in famine. Even in the face of death, starvation, and dehydration, the people continued to give their allegiance to false gods. You would think that today with so many hurricanes, floods, earthquakes, tornados, and volcanic eruptions, someone would ask, "Do you think God is trying to tell us something?"

Make no mistake, everyone knew who Elijah was. Like Martin Luther, he was willing to nail his convictions to the door. Like Paul, he was willing to stand toe-to-toe before political leaders and demand they change their ways. Alexander Whyte said Elijah was a man who was always passionate about something. What are you passionate about?

His life was characterized by a burning desire to see the people return to the one true God. He was indignant at the compromise that surrounded him. The man with fire in his bones would call down fire because the honor of God was at stake. Elijah never faced a situation when he did not believe that God had an answer. Not only is he a model for a true prophet, but he is also a model for prevailing prayer.

Before the showdown on the mountain, there was a season of praying. As you read through the story of Elijah's confrontation with the prophets of Baal, you realize that in prayer Elijah understood this was not about his being right but about the Lord God of Israel being exalted. He had a backbone, but he got it from bended knees.

The story is told of a man who stood at the grave of John Wesley, whose preaching shook England and led to a national revival, and said, "Do it again, Lord, do it again." I've stood in an old Quaker cemetery outside Greensboro, North Carolina, by the tombstone of my hero Vance Havner, a twentieth-century revivalist and prophet, and asked God to use me as an instrument of revival.

C. H. Spurgeon wrote, "If you are sure it is a right thing for which you are asking, plead now, plead at noon, plead at night, plead on. With cries and tears spread out your case. Order your arguments. Back up your pleas with reasons."[2]

Once you've prayed and have a word from God, stand on it. Walk onto the battlefield wearing your spiritual armor. Stand firm on the fact that God has heard your prayers and honors His promises. March into battle, no longer content to sit on the sidelines and give your family or the nation to the devil by default.

I hear folks say, "I almost said something." Say something! Be bold! The early church didn't move the world by staying in their holy huddle. They prayed and then went forth to share the message of the cross. Even when they were persecuted, they just prayed for more boldness.

"Behold, Elijah is here." His presence changed the conversation and demanded a decision. I find it funny (and sad) when I walk into a situation and people change their conversations because the "preacher" is here. I don't want the conversation to change because I'm the preacher. I want it to change because they recognize me as a man of God. Let me ask you, does the conversation ever change when you walk into the room? Are there jokes they will not tell and things they will not say in your presence?

Elijah showed up and said, "Tell the king and that woman, I'm here. Tell the false prophets, I'm here. Tell your so-called gods, I'm here" (see 1 Kings 18:17–19). No one gets away with rebellion against God. Name the nation or the empire that maintained its domination after giving themselves to violence, godless idolatry, sensuality, and immorality. Whether it is the Philistines, Assyrians, Greeks, Romans, Huns, Nazis, Communists, or the terrorists, all have or will pass off the scene. If America doesn't have a Mount Carmel moment, we too will fall.

Our nation is clearly worshipping false gods at false altars. We can't blame the younger generation for this because it has happened on our watch. Everything has deteriorated in our lifetime. We've fought wars to maintain freedom, but we are in bondage to the spirit of compromise and complacency.

Our land is filled with altars to false gods. We bow before everything from an all-you-can-eat buffet (in a world of poverty and starvation) to the gods of fame and fortune. We treat celebrities like gods. We bow down to politicians who appear to hold the power of life and death in their hands. We sell our souls for entertainment, technology, and science. We have everything except God. Before the older generation points fingers at the younger generation, just remember, it happened on *our* watch.

We worship at the altar of political correctness and nonoffensive preaching. We have little appetite for the meat of the Word and a call to the cross.

I'm sure someone tried to tell Elijah to be more positive. The problem is that you can't be positive about something that is negative. You can't call disaster a success. You can't applaud compromise as commitment. We must have the courage to "come apart" and "be holy." Christianity is not a cafeteria line where we pick and choose what we want. "If the Lord is God, follow Him."

Elijah was not the troubler of Israel as Ahab deemed. He was the only one standing between Israel and certain, lasting judgment. A man of courage will disturb the peace of status quo. He will call his friends to stand up. He is resolute and not ashamed to say it. Ahab was the troublemaker; Elijah was the troubleshooter.

We live in an age when godlessness abounds at every hand. If America is going to avoid being a twenty-first-century version of the book of Judges, we're going to have to find men and women who will stand up without hesitation or reservation for things eternal.

At this late and dark hour, we need one to show up who will speak for God. Luther showed up and confronted the corruption of the established church. When politics and morals were at low ebb in Great Britain, God raised up Tyndale, Whitfield, and Wesley to turn the tide and initiate a great revival. When America needed a man to stand up, Jonathan Edwards answered the call. Billy Sunday stood up in the days when alcohol was destroying the land. When is someone going to stand up in the twenty-first century and say, "That's enough!"

What is stopping us from having a move of God today? If we make up our minds to follow Christ fully and to bend the knee to no one but our Lord, we can see the tide turn. But it won't happen on our current course.

On Mount Carmel, Elijah threw down the gauntlet. The game was on. It was time for a spiritual smack-down. Three groups gathered that day: the devoted servant of God, Elijah; the dedicated followers of Baal; and the undecided masses. James said an indecisive man is unstable in all his ways (1:8). It may have looked like Elijah was alone, but the man of God is never alone. One plus God equals a majority. "The One who is in you is greater than the one who is in the world" (1 John 4:4).

Elijah demanded a choice be made. He determined three-and-a-half years was long enough to reach a decision. The false gods had not come through, and they weren't going to. Why the delay? How long will you hesitate (see 1 Kings 18:21)? The word *hesitate* means "to halt or limp along." How much time do you need? How many sermons do you have to hear? Man up. The time is now to make up your mind. Have the courage to pick a side.

Remember the plague of frogs in Egypt? The frogs took over, and finally Pharaoh called Moses in and said, "Get rid of the frogs." Moses told him he would, but he tossed the ball back in Pharaoh's court as to the timing. Pharaoh said, "Tomorrow." One more night with the frogs. I'm miserable, but before I get rid of my misery, can I sleep with it one more time (see Exod. 8:8ff)?

Elijah demanded a commitment. He gave the prophets of Baal the chance to go first. If they were smart and had paid attention during those three years of drought, they would have repented. But they didn't. They cried out all day long. They cut themselves, chanted, and shouted, and nothing happened. False gods are like that; they never come through when you need them.

Elijah let them go on and even mocked them. Finally he declared enough was enough. He started rebuilding the altar and called on God to answer (1 Kings 18:30–39). Elijah prayed. All the high points of his life came as the result of the effectual prayer of a righteous man. He prayed it wouldn't rain, and it didn't. He prayed for fire to fall, and it did. He prayed it would rain again, and it poured. You can't impact your generation if you aren't willing to have a showdown and live with the consequences.

Elijah called on God to answer by fire. When the fire fell, the people got it. It reminded them of their history with Jehovah: the burning bush, Mount Sinai, the pillar of fire. Fire was a symbol of the presence and power of God. The fire fell and consumed everything. When God's fire falls in revival, it will burn away the dross and junk that has hindered us. Then Elijah prayed for rain, and the rain came and revived the land.

I'm an advocate for the public invitation. I believe we need to confess publicly where we stand with Jesus. We need the fire to fall again. It will fall when God finds men at an altar, pouring their hearts out in prayer for themselves and their families. It's time, young men, to start an altar, to have a place where you go to spend time with God in prayer and the Word. Where are the altars in our churches? We have steps but no altars. Where is the mourner's bench? We have moving lights, but we need men moving to the altar to repent and repair that which has been neglected.

In our weekly worship services, I am seeing an increasing number of men in their twenties and thirties coming to the altar to do business with God. There on their knees they settle accounts, find forgiveness, and gain courage. There they give themselves as a living sacrifice (see Rom. 12:1).

Vance Havner was the only man who reminded me of an Old Testament prophet. When he showed up in a church, he thinned out the crowd. His call was to preach to the remnant to stir themselves up. That's my call in this chapter. It is my prayer that God would use the example of Elijah to make us courageous enough to tell the truth and confront the culture.

If we ever needed that fire and that flood, now is the time. But we are not ready for a showdown on Carmel. . . . We are out for summit conferences, not confrontations. . . . Some say: "We don't have time to put on a revival in our conventions." *We don't have time for anything else!* It is too late! Some will say, "We are here to attend to business." *What greater business is there than to rebuild broken altars, and offer the sacrifice of penitence, person and praise?* When we do that and call on God in holy desperation, if we ever do, then the fire will fall, and there will be the sound of abundance of rain.

Evangelism is not enough; the first items on God's program for the church today are repentance, confession of sin, cleansing and separation from the world, submission to Christ's Lordship, and the filling of the Spirit, but we politely dodge all that in our convocations. Elijah did not call a conference of Ahab, Jezebel, the priests of Baal, and Obadiah; he stood alone. And yet he was not alone, for seven thousand had not bowed to Baal. Today there is still a remnant and a cloud the size of a man's hand.[3]

Whether alone at your own private altar or at an altar in your church, find a place, get on your knees, and don't get up until you've resolved to be the person God needs in this hour. Stay until the fire of God burns in your heart. Stay until the rivers of living water flow through you. Linger long enough so that when you get up, others will look at you and say, "_____ is here!"

Courage is the tenacity to bring about change; determination is the persistence to continue to see that change through to the end. Who will be first?

Chapter 8

THE COURAGE TO FACE CRITICISM

---

*"So I sent messengers to them, saying, 'I am doing a
great work and cannot come down. Why should the
work cease while I leave it and go down to you?'"*
(Nehemiah 6:3)

*"I will forgive those who have wronged me and
reconcile with those I have wronged. I will walk in
integrity as a man answerable to God,
and I will seek to honor God, obey His Word,
and do His will."*

—The Resolution, *Courageous*

N o one is immune from criticism. It comes with breathing.
I'd rather be criticized for doing something than nothing.
I have dedicated this book to my friend Daniel Simmons.
Daniel is the pastor of Mt. Zion Baptist Church here in Albany,
the largest African-American church in our region. We have
worked together on many projects through the years—and not
without criticism. He and I have received more than our fair

share of criticism and attacks for partnering to build bridges and work toward reconciliation.

People in both communities have taken pot shots at us. We've both been the subject of caustic comments on the editorial page and have given the bigots and racists a great deal of angst. Yet because we were willing to take a stand, other churches in our area are now seeking ways to partner across racial lines. It's not always easy to overcome the critics, but it's worth it.

Because of Daniel's courage, two unique ministries have been birthed out of Mt. Zion. Their Boys to Men Ministry is a bi-weekend youth development program designed to assist young males in their maturation to adulthood. The ministry provides exposure to character-building and life-fulfilling situations. It further provides leadership skills, motivation, academic preparation, and the opportunity to increase the esteem of all its participants. The men of Mt. Zion are making a difference in the next generation.

In addition to this ministry, the Mt. Zion Summer Youth Academy for Boys serves as a mentoring program for boys, ages nine to fourteen. It addresses the academic and social needs of young boys, transforming them into young men. As a result of the experiences of the boys while in this ministry, former participants often return and work with boys in the program.

We have a serious gang problem in Albany, Georgia. As we began working on *Courageous*, it was clear to us in dealing with the issues of fathers that we needed to address the consequences of fatherlessness. Daniel's passion and ministry have reinforced that this was the right decision.

A critic would say, "What's the use?" But Daniel has led

his church to try to change the culture. Others might say, "What difference can one church make? The problem is out of control." The pastor and people of Mt. Zion have said, "That may be the way it is, but we aren't going to accept it."

Because of his courageous leadership, we asked Daniel to play the role of a strategic mentor and father figure for one of the officers in the film. The work of Daniel and the congregation at Mt. Zion is keeping young men out of gangs and off the streets. I believe that one day some young man is going to come out of that ministry and make a difference in the lives of many.

Teddy Roosevelt certainly met his share of critics, but he faced them head-on. He said:

> It is not the critic who counts; not the man who points out how the strong man stumbled or where the doer of deeds could have done them better. The credit belongs to the man who is actually in the arena; whose face is marred by dust and sweat and blood; who strives valiantly; who errs and comes short again and again, because there is no effort without error and shortcoming; who does actually try to do the deed; who knows the great enthusiasm, the great devotion and spends himself in a worthy cause; who, at the worst, if he fails, at least fails while daring greatly.
>
> Far better it is to dare mighty things, to win glorious triumphs even though checkered by failure than to rank with those poor spirits who neither enjoy nor suffer much because they live in the gray twilight that knows neither victory nor defeat.[1]

Have you ever seen a monument erected to a critic? When the critic throws stones, the visionary should take them and build a wall. Then if the critic wants to see what you've built, charge him admission to get through the gate.

Great ideas and leaders have a common enemy—the critic. Criticism is one of the enemy's favorite flaming arrows. He is the accuser of the brethren. Satan will attack those who threaten his strategy as the god of this age. If you stick your neck out, expect the enemy to take note of you.

I can tell you I've faced my share of opposition. I've got the scars to prove it. While some of the sweetest people I've known were God's people, some of the meanest people I've ever met have been in the church. (Please note that I do not assume the critic is a child of God.)

You may be part of a church where people seek power or want to run the church. Their name is legion, and they breed. You can't let those kinds of people derail you or cause you to give up on the church.

I challenge you to live the kind of life that causes people to disbelieve your critics when they speak ill of you. In my Bible beside Galatians 2:20 I have written, "Dead to flattery and flattening." We have to be both. The fact is this: those who can, act; those who can't, criticize. Find someone complaining about the way the ball bounces, and you'll probably find the person who never picked it up, or worse, dropped it.

With the success of Sherwood Pictures, we've had our share of flattery and flattening. Some think we're the greatest thing since sliced bread, while others think we're the worst thing since the Black Plague. The truth is somewhere in the middle. We don't show our films to movie critics for reviews because we don't make movies for critics. One person said to me, "If you don't show your movies to critics, people could assume they are lame or cheesy." I responded, "We don't care what critics think." We make movies to reach people for an audience of One. Our standard is not Hollywood; it's Him.

As we were filming *Courageous*, I found myself in a huddle with four of the five men who play male leads in the movie: Kevin Downes, Ken Bevel, Robert Amaya, and Alex Kendrick. We had an eyeball-to-eyeball discussion about how recognition and fame can feed pride. We asked God to deal with us if anything in our lives would hinder God using the film.

Praise and criticism come and go. Pleasing God is all that matters. To reply to a nasty remark with another nasty remark is like trying to remove dirt with mud. But to believe someone who feeds your fleshly pride is also dangerous. We have to avoid both. Praise undeserved is poison in disguise. Thomas Brooks wrote, "Flattery is the devil's invisible net."

With the increased awareness of Sherwood Pictures, we have been a target at times. I remind myself of what D. L. Moody said when questioned about his methods of evangelism, "I like my way of doing it better than your way of not doing it." It's not that we aren't willing to learn, but we make movies for a greater purpose. We receive constructive criticism from people who love us, partner with us, and believe in us. Unknown critics and unsigned e-mails are never read. Why? Those opinions don't matter.

When I think of the courage to face criticism, my attention is drawn to Nehemiah. His story is set some time after Daniel and others had been taken captive to Babylon. The captivity lasted seventy years, and eventually Persia became the world power. When Artaxerxes assumed the throne of Persia he allowed Ezra to return to Jerusalem, and later Nehemiah followed. These two led a great restoration of the walls of Jerusalem and a revival among the people.

Nehemiah is one of the great leaders in Scripture. His story is told in black-and-white. He pulled no punches, and he never backed down from a conflict. He named his critics. He boldly declared, "I am doing a great work and cannot come down" (6:3).

Nehemiah was also a man of prayer. His plans were birthed in prayer. His responses came in a prayer environment. Who he was in prayer prepared him to be who he was in public. Nehemiah's public life was empowered by his private life. Prayer was fundamental not supplemental. His work was bathed in prayer (see 1:4, 6; 2:4; 4:4, 9; 5:19; 6:14; 13:14, 22, 29).

If you do anything great for God, you are going to need prayer support. Every project completed, victory won, and obstacle overcome in my ministry has been the result of prayer. The power of a praying church cannot be measured.

Nehemiah was a great man in an influential position serving the king. He could not stay quiet while Jerusalem lay in ruins. Therefore, he was honest in his praying. Nehemiah wept, mourned, and fasted. He prayed day and night on behalf of the people of God (see Neh. 1:4ff). He was honest about the apostasy of the people, and he told God what the opposition was trying to do to derail the work.

The city of God was in ruins; the walls were in shambles. There was no king, prophet, or priest to stand for God.

Nonetheless, God orchestrated events to move Nehemiah, a cupbearer to the king of Persia, out of exile (1:11).

Nehemiah wasn't merely a cupbearer; he was also a builder. Nehemiah had a God-given vision, as the city needed walls if it was going to withstand enemy attacks. The ruined walls had been a problem for years, but something had to be done. Nehemiah was God's man to do it, though the task wouldn't come without difficulty.

We need walls in our own lives. It's not courageous just to "trust the Lord." We need to put feet to our prayers. We need to build four walls in our lives: faith, courage, integrity, and prayer. Surrounding our hearts with these four walls of defense will allow us to stand in an evil day.

Fortunately the people embraced the vision and followed Nehemiah. They were ready to rebuild the wall. But remember, not everyone will be happy when you start to do something great for God. There are people, even in the Christian community, that want you to fail. Jealousy and envy will lead people to attack you. Never let a loser tell you how to win!

Critics will never be an endangered species, but we should ask God to create a spiritual environment where they can't breed. If Nehemiah had caved into critics, the wall would have never been rebuilt.

You must have the courage to withstand the critic. I've had my share. Every leader does. By God's grace we have an environment at Sherwood where we are not a breeding ground for cynics and critics. At the same time I know we are one malcontent away from someone trying to stir things up. So we pray and practice unity on every front.

For Nehemiah, Sanballat was one of those guys who just wouldn't stop. He wouldn't move his church letter or see the error of his ways. Scripture clearly reveals his attitude: "When Sanballat the Horonite and Tobiah the Ammonite official heard that someone had come to seek the well-being of the Israelites, they were greatly displeased" (2:10).

These guys were ticked off. Critics make three kinds of statements: it can't be done; it shouldn't be done; it won't be done. When you walk with God, you'll anger those who don't. The way you react to criticism will reveal if you are courageous or intimidated.

I know men who want to be leaders, but they're afraid of criticism. They live with the fear of man, and they will never build a wall or leave a legacy. A heresy floating around says if you are doing God's will, then everything will work out without a hitch. Where is the chapter and verse to back up such illogical and unbiblical thinking? The fact is that change makes some people angry, and the anger can be devilish.

If you are a leader, you are going to face critics. To avoid criticism, say nothing, do nothing, and be nothing. If you are doing God's will, expect opposition. Face the task with tenacity, and face your problems in prayer (see 1 John 5:4).

Why did Nehemiah receive such hostile criticism? Because if he was successful, Sanballat's economic security would be jeopardized. If Jerusalem was rebuilt, it would attract business and cut into Samaria's economic supremacy. It was Sanballat's strategy to "lower their self-esteem, weaken their resolve, and destroy their morale"[2] so he could keep things status quo. Critics only act in their own best interest.

We have a section in our local newspaper called the

Squawkbox, a place where cowards can anonymously leave a few sentences of criticism or praise. (The criticism outweighs the praise one hundred to one.) I've been the target a few times. My motives have been questioned, and our church has been attacked. I choose not to respond because it wouldn't do any good. Proverbs says a harsh word stirs up anger. If you really want to get them, don't respond and sic the Lord on them (see Neh. 4:4–6).

Nehemiah met the opposition with prayer, but he also kept working. After you've prayed, go back to work. The enemy will work to get you to start arguing. Agonizing and organizing are two sides of the same coin. We work and we wait. We watch and we pray.

In *Courageous* the group of sheriff officers makes a commitment to take responsibility as godly husbands and fathers. Unfortunately we live in a culture where more and more men are bailing out on their responsibilities and passively standing by as their wives and children stumble along, begging for someone to lead them. In the film Adam Mitchell makes a speech representative of the vow that all the men have made.

A father should love his children and seek to win their hearts. He should protect them, discipline them, and teach them about God. He should model how to walk with integrity and treat others with respect and should call out his children to become responsible men and women who will live their lives for what matters in eternity. Some men may hear this and mock it or ignore it, but I tell you that as a father, you are accountable to God for the position of influence He has given you.

You can't afford to fall asleep at the wheel, only to wake up one day and realize that your job or your hobbies have no eternal value, but the souls of your children do. Some men will hear this and agree with it but have no resolve to live it out. They will end up living for themselves and waste the opportunity to leave a legacy for the next generation.

But there are some men who, regardless of our mistakes in the past and regardless of what our fathers did not do for us, will give the strength of our arms and the rest of our days to love God with all that we are and teach our children to do the same. And we are inviting any man whose heart is courageous and willing to join us in this resolution. The world wants the hearts of your children, and they will fight for their devotion.

Opposition can take a hundred forms. Sanballat and Tobiah first ridiculed Nehemiah and mocked the Jews (Neh. 4:1–3). As you continue to read, you see that the opposition began to mock God's people. The Hebrew word for *mock* means to stammer or to stutter. The critics kept repeating their negative comments, hoping to discourage the people and their work. Chuck Swindoll writes, "Part of the unwritten job requirements for every leader is the ability to handle criticism. That's part of the leadership package. If you never get criticized, chances are you aren't getting anything done."[3]

I've met the relatives of Sanballat and Tobiah. You'll find them on every expedition, adventure, and project. They not only threw verbal barbs, but they also mocked the work that had already been done. Critics don't need a reason to criticize. Oscar Wilde asked, "What is a cynic? A man who knows the price of everything and the value of nothing."[4]

If criticism doesn't work, they will start to threaten you. Nehemiah's opponents became furious and fought the work at every turn (4:7–8). Nehemiah's response? "We prayed to our God and stationed a guard because of them day and night" (4:9).

Watch and work. Stay focused. These critics didn't just criticize the workers; they challenged the Lord God. Those who oppose the work of God are opposing God Himself. Nehemiah made sure the people stayed focused. He kept them on task. His first response was prayer. His second was to set watchmen on the wall.

Scripture reminds us to be alert, to watch and pray, and to stand firm. We need to stand strong when people are trying to knock us down or stop the work we are doing. The greater the progress in the work, the greater the criticism. The more successful the work, the more intense the attacks.

The enemies of Nehemiah began to use a little psychological warfare. They worked to instill discouragement and fear in the hearts of the people (Neh. 4:14 and 6:9, 13). They threatened to tell King Artaxerxes that Nehemiah was a traitor, but their threats didn't rattle Nehemiah. Remember, he had been cupbearer to the king and had already earned his trust.

If you are going to face criticism and survive it, you must be determined, steadfast, confident, and bold. One of the great tests for a leader is the ability to persevere. Most of us quit too soon. We let the critics win because we lack the tenacity to finish the task.

Critics want to convince you they have greater support on their side than you do. God has never sided with or blessed a critic. The devil rejoices when we buckle under pressure and when we blink in a showdown. Nehemiah handed out swords, placed the people in position, and kept working. "When our enemies heard that we knew their scheme and that God had frustrated it, every one of us returned to his own work on the wall" (4:15).

If you want to drive a critic crazy, keep doing what God told you to do. You can't answer every accusation, but you can build a wall. Nothing troubles a troublemaker like seeing the work go on. In his book *Stuff Christians Like*, Jonathan Acuff writes, "Hate from others is like moss, it can only grow on stagnant objects. The motion of following your calling repels hate."

Roy Laurin writes, "Never stop working to fight. Be ready to fight and repel the invader but always keep up the work. A man's greatest defense is the work he is doing. If he constantly answers the attacks made on him he cannot work and if he does not work, he will not be able to fulfill the purpose of his life."[5]

Paul asked, "If God is for us, who is against us?" (Rom. 8:31). Nehemiah never lost sight of his goal and completed the wall in fifty-two days. How? The people had a mind to work. They were inspired by Nehemiah's courage, and Nehemiah's work was vindicated. Every move of his critics was met by faith, prayer, and preparation. God gave him the strategies to match the attacks of the enemy. At every turn Nehemiah had an answer for the need of the hour.

In chapter 6 Nehemiah's critics tried to trap him by

appealing for a private meeting, but Nehemiah was too smart and too wise to fall for that trap. "'Come, let's meet together in the villages of the Ono Valley.' But they were planning to harm me" (6:1–2).

Nehemiah was quick to respond. "I am doing a great work and cannot come down. Why should the work cease while I leave it and go down to you?" (6:3–4). They came at him "four times" with "the same proposal." The courageous man needs to discern between someone who is sincere and someone with an agenda.

You must have the courage to confront critics. They can't be ignored, and they won't change because it's not in their DNA. Most critics are either jealous, threatened, or uninformed. The only reason they have influence is because we have let them. If we are going to be people of courage, the critic can no longer control our lives.

It's easy to run from critics. For the last twenty plus years I've pastored the same church. I decided to plant my flag and give my life to one place. Running would have been easier, but staying was God's plan for my life. Today I am blessed to pastor a church that walks in unity.

I'm amazed by the way this congregation accepts my leadership and believes in the vision God has given me. I'm grateful for the men and women who pray daily for me. I love the young people who sit down front in the worship services. I am blessed with deacons "full of faith and the Holy Spirit" (Acts 6:5). There is so much about Sherwood to love.

I must admit there were times I let a handful spoil it for me. No matter who you are or what you do, not everyone is going to agree with you. Just do what God says and let someone else worry about the critics. Be careful who you listen to. I have a handful of men who have permission to speak into my life when they see something that shouldn't be there. They tell me if I've said something inappropriate in a message. They confront me. The key is they love me unconditionally and want the best for me. I'm grateful to have Spirit-filled men who can reprove, rebuke, correct, and teach when needed.

What happened because Nehemiah didn't stop the work to respond to critics? The wall was completed in fifty-two days. My advice to you is simple: never let someone who has done nothing tell you how to do anything.

Chapter 9

THE COURAGE TO
STIR UP THE FIRE

---

*"Therefore, I remind you to keep ablaze the gift
of God that is in you through the laying on of
my hands. For God has not given us a spirit of
fearfulness, but one of power, love, and sound
judgment. So don't be ashamed of the testimony
about our Lord." (2 Timothy 1:6–8)*

*"I'm thirty-seven years old and have never met my
biological father. . . . A man in my neighborhood
named William Barrett mentored me as a teenager.
He taught me about God. Every Father's Day,
he's the one I call."*

—Nathan Hayes, *Courageous*

W hatever I am today for God is largely the result of
people who invested in my life. Whether they were
Sunday school teachers growing up, my youth minister,
laymen I've had the privilege of serving with, or heroes in my
life, all have impacted, molded, and shaped me into who I am
today.

One man in particular who impacted my life was Frank
Favazza. Frank was a layman and a homebuilder by trade.
In reality he was a mentor to untold numbers of men along
the way. When I was a starving seminary student, Frank
would take me out to lunch, usually to the best steak house in
Kansas City, and buy me a meal. It was his way of getting my
undivided attention for several hours as he discipled me and
taught me out of the Word of God. His life was his message.

In Frank's home were dozens of Bibles. He would take
a Bible and go from Genesis to Revelation studying one
particular word. Whether the word was *faith, truth, grace,* or
a dozen others, he wanted to read what God said about that
subject in its context. I wish I owned one of those Bibles today.

In my twenties I was introduced to one of the great
mentors of the last fifty years, Max Barnett. Max was the
head of the BSU at the University of Oklahoma. Actually
Max was a disciple maker cleverly disguised as a BSU director.
Thousands have been impacted by his life and ministry.

Investing in others takes time. If we are going to raise a
generation of giants for God, we need to reevaluate how we
spend our time (see 1 John 2:12–14; 2 John 7). Those who are
farther along in our journey must seek out and call out younger
men and women to be wholehearted followers of Christ.
Today's youth are more conscious of the presence of men than
the presence of God. I believe millions are waiting to hear
someone challenge them and stir them up to greater things.

There is a bland predictability about Christianity today. It
seems we are the only believers on the planet who are afraid
to stand up for what they believe. While the world will never
compromise, we compromise easily and often.

Proverbs 25:26 says, "A righteous person who yields to the wicked is like a muddied spring or a polluted well." We claim to be individuals, but we look and sound like clones of the culture. No one seems to be in the mood to be different. I'm not talking about being weird; I am talking about making an impact. It's time to raise the bar.

The first time I read the resolution scene in *Courageous*, every fiber of my being wanted to stand up and cheer. It's a call to be courageous, take action, and return to the principles of godliness. When we take our commitments seriously, we make significant inroads into the lives of others.

Paul reminds us "to walk worthy of the calling you have received" (Eph. 4:1). John said we are to be in the world but not of the world. That doesn't mean we are to avoid non-Christians, nor does it mean we become a chameleon. It means we've been delivered from a desire to follow the attitudes of the culture. What Jesus said about taking up the cross and dying to self is not in fine print; it's headline news in the Gospels.

Paul's words to Timothy about the last days reads like the front page of the newspaper or any news site on the Internet.

But know this: Difficult times will come in the last days. For people will be lovers of self, lovers of money, boastful, proud, blasphemers, disobedient to parents, ungrateful, unholy, unloving, irreconcilable, slanderers, without self-control, brutal, without love for what is good, traitors, reckless, conceited, lovers of pleasure rather than lovers of God, holding to the form of godliness but denying its power. Avoid these people! (2 Tim. 3:1–5)

How do we stand in difficult days? We can't do it in our own strength. We need the Holy Spirit to empower us. We need others to encourage and equip us. We know the need; we need someone to model the *how* for us. We need to see living witnesses of the power of the Holy Spirit to radically change lives. We need to be stirred up. Emotions will pass, but we need to be stirred in the depths of our being. We can get stirred up at an event, but I'm talking about a lifelong process of growing and maturing.

Now is the time. In a recent sermon at Sherwood, Tom Elliff asked a series of pointed questions: If not now, when? If not you, who? If not here, where? If not by prayer, then how? Jesus calls us to a narrow road, the cross life, a radical new way of thinking. His call is to "be with Him" and to "follow Him." We are to "learn from Him." As infants we need help. We can't feed ourselves, change ourselves, or walk on our own. We need someone to carry us until we are able to take care of ourselves.

We need mentors and role models who will show us how they live out their faith. We need people to pour into our lives who haven't lost their way. We must have others in our lives who will not allow us to accept average or status quo as the norm.

Much of what I see targeted at young adults is pabulum, watered-down Christianity, if it could even be called Christianity at all. With all the talent and technology we have, you would think we could figure out what truth is. Unfortunately some of the leading voices to the younger generation are more concerned about being cool than Christlike. They pat themselves on the back for the things they are able to do because of their "freedom" in Christ. They speak little of the cross, dying to self, and being a world changer.

I'm discovering that the harder I preach and the higher I set the demands, the more response I'm getting out of young people and young adults. They are nauseated by compromise and apathy within the church. They've figured out there's something more. They are longing for someone to point them in the right direction.

Over the last twenty years we have had men's accountability groups led by our staff. In addition, many men's groups have been formed for prayer and accountability. Recently we started an intentional discipling ministry for men in our church. Each staff member is taking a small group of men through *Masterlife* on Tuesday mornings. We are seeking to intentionally impact men who will impact other men (see 2 Tim. 2:2). The potential to start a heavenly fire in the hearts of men is in our midst if we fan the flames.

In his book *The Table of Inwardness*, Calvin Miller tells the story of an antique wooden box from the nineteenth century that had a lid with large red and black letters on it which read: DANGER! DYNAMITE! But Miller wrote, "The last time I saw it, it was filled with common paraphernalia that could be found in any workroom." The box designated for dynamite and power was filled with nothing more than flammable junk.

This illustration defines our problem. We say we have power, but far too many accept defeat as normal. We have the Spirit within us, but we live in fear of our foe. We talk about dynamite, but we are duds. While we affirm the book of Acts, we are light-years removed from any evidence of such power. The leaders of the work of God in Acts weren't, by and large, professional preachers; they were laymen. Peter was a fisherman by trade, and Paul was a tent maker.

Fatherless children, broken homes, single-parent moms—their voices are crying out for someone to step up and help them with their kids. Churches are in need of godly men who will be unwavering in their preaching. The church has something to offer that the YMCA and Boys and Girls Clubs can't: the life changing power of the gospel. When we see opportunities, we need to seize them, even if they require us to readjust our schedule.

I'm thinking of a friend who is the pastor of a large church. He and his wife have just taken in a twenty-four-year-old homeless man and are helping him get his GED. He sent me a note telling me he had shown the young man *Facing the Giants* to encourage him in his journey.

We see this principle in the life of one of the characters portrayed in *Courageous*, Shane Fuller. As an officer, he paraded around as a committed believer, good father, and respectable coworker. However, it is later revealed that he has been hiding his true identity. All was not as it appeared to be. His poor choices nearly cost him his family, but a fellow officer, Adam, steps in to help him win back the heart of his son. Adam becomes a mentor for the young boy as he struggles through the consequences of his father's poor decisions.

One of my prayers is that God would raise up mentors and disciple makers. A mentor is a role model, trusted counselor, or guide. We find a biblical model for mentoring: Moses mentored Joshua, Barnabas poured his life into John Mark, and Paul cared for Timothy as his own son. Of course, Jesus called and taught His disciples. He invested in them, knowing He would one day leave them.

Paul was concerned about the future of the gospel. He was passing the torch to young Timothy who was, at times, fearful and timid. I'm amazed that from the talent pool that was probably available to Paul, he would choose Timothy. Paul selected a young man in his thirties who wasn't in the best health. The apostle reminded him to stir up the gift of God within him and not let the world intimidate him.

Paul poured his life into Timothy. The old apostle knew the fires of the early days of the church could go out if the next generation did not take seriously what had been entrusted to them. Paul called Timothy to stand above the crowd (see 2 Tim. 1:5–8; 2:1–7, 15; 3:1; 4:1–5).

Paul knew the day was coming when people wouldn't put up with sound doctrine. He didn't say they wouldn't enjoy it or appreciate it; he said they wouldn't endure it or put up with it. He wanted to raise up a generation that would be able to digest the meat of the Word. He didn't want the body of Christ trying to live off cotton candy.

I love junk food. It tastes better than healthy food. Who wants broccoli when you can eat a Butterfinger? But if you live on junk food, you'll die because of it. Ron Dunn said, "History teaches us, the farther every generation takes us is one step further from the source of the flame."

Paul was coming down the home stretch of his life. He wanted to make sure he left the gospel in good hands. Paul mentioned three men in his letter to Timothy. They are pictures of men you know or possibly even you (2 Tim. 4:9ff).

First Paul mentioned Demas. At one point he had been on Paul's staff. Think about what kind of guy you had to be to make it on Paul's staff. But things had changed. "Demas because he loved this present world, has deserted me and gone to Thessalonica" (v. 10). Demas had the same potential as Timothy, and maybe that's why Paul mentioned him. He didn't want to see timid Timothy go down the same path. What a contrast we see here: Paul was in prison facing death, and Demas moved to the big city to live the life of ease. He didn't want to pay the price. He had the "let me first" attitude (Luke 9).

Then there was John Mark. He had accompanied Paul on his first missionary journey, but he got homesick and left before the work was completed. On the second journey, Paul and Barnabas went their separate ways over whether or not to take John Mark. Now, years later, Paul wrote to Timothy, "Bring Mark with you, for he is useful to me in the ministry" (2 Tim. 4:11). Apparently Barnabas made a minister out of John Mark. The word *service* is the same word for the task John Mark was given on the first missionary journey. Failure doesn't have to be final. God redeemed John Mark's failures.

God has allowed me to be a "father" to several "sons" in the ministry. My love for them is deeper than I can express. I've ordained them and tried to put the fear of God in them. I try to invest in those young men. Although all of us are busy, many of them call, text, or e-mail me to seek wisdom about how to handle a situation.

One of those guys is Garrett Grubbs, our youth minister at Sherwood. He shared the following:

Michael became my pastor when I was eleven years old. Twenty years later I serve alongside him as the student minister at Sherwood. I have been saved, baptized, married, and ordained under Michael's ministry. He has walked with my wife and me on the mountaintops and through the valleys of life. We consider Michael as a spiritual father. He has walked with our family through the loss of two children and two failed adoptions, and he has celebrated with us through the adoption of our son this year.

Michael has taught me that success in ministry is not the approval of man but obedience to Christ. Michael has taught us to glean wisdom from men that have lived out the faith well. One of the ways he helps sharpen us is by sending us books and messages that have shaped his life. His investment in my life can't be measured!

One of my dad's chores growing up was to put wood on the fire in the mornings. He had to stoke the coals, blow on them, and add a little kindling to the fire before he put the logs on. That's what Paul urged Timothy to do. He called him to "keep ablaze the gift of God" (2 Tim. 1:6). God is not going to do for us what we are supposed to do ourselves. There is a difference between God's work and man's responsibility.

He was to rekindle the fire of God, not his own fire. All these exhortations from Paul were the outgrowth of this one command: kindle afresh! It could be that Timothy was in danger of getting into a rut. He wasn't making the progress Paul thought he should be making.

We are lacking people who are stirred up. God never wastes words. He never says to a man who is awake, "Wake up!" He never says to a man standing up, "Stand up!" or to a man lying down, "Lie down!" Nor does he say to a man who is already on fire, "Kindle afresh!" Paul called for commitment to an "above and beyond" mentality. The devil works to convince us that those early days of reckless abandonment to Christ need to be toned down. Paul reminded Timothy that he needed a burning heart.

Many of us have bailed out on God over less significant things than what Timothy faced. He was facing growing persecution, possible imprisonment, and constant attacks from the Judaizers and Gnostics. We lose our fire too easily. We allow the fear of man to extinguish our fire. We worry about what others think or how they will talk about us at the coffee shop. We worry about success and job security and follow the path of compromise.

There are many strange fires today. The prosperity gospel will extinguish the true fire and only works if you live in a materialistic, self-centered society. We're also faced with the strange fire of a watered-down gospel and a compromised church. Another strange fire is "spirituality." We see Oprah and other celebrities embracing it, most not even understanding it's a hodgepodge of various religions, all leading to a dead end. It's the faith of a postmodern, relative truth world. The man of courage will long for the fire of God in his bones.

Timothy didn't need a shot of adrenaline or enthusiasm or a pregame pep talk; he needed unction from the Holy Spirit. Like most of us, as time went on, Timothy's emotions began to wane. Life can wear you down or make you fearful. Timothy faced opposition inside and outside the church. Maybe he was close to burnout. Paul encouraged him: "Kindle afresh." Literally, keep the fire alive, fan the embers into a flame, and don't let the fire die out.

J. Wilbur Chapman said, "Anything that diminishes my vision for Christ, or takes away my taste for Bible study, or cramps my prayer life or makes Christian work difficult, is wrong for me and I must, as a Christian, turn away from it."

Recently I observed a large youth conference, and what I saw broke my heart. The young people came filing in, heads down, many of them listening to their iPods. They looked like they were walking into a funeral, not into a conference with a band and great speaker. We need to call them to step up. The times demand that we call students to a new level of commitment.

Because of movies like *Gladiator*, we are all familiar with the brutality of the Roman games. A courageous monk named Telemachus lived in a day when the games were still popular. He went to Rome and followed the crowds into the Colosseum to see what he, as one individual, might be able to do to stop the games. When the first pair of gladiators came out and drew their swords, he leaped into the arena and ran between the two fighters and cried out, "In the name of our Master, stop fighting!" The gladiators hesitated, but the furious, bloodthirsty crowd stampeded into the arena and beat the monk to death. Upon seeing his dead body, the crowd withdrew as a silence fell over that massive Colosseum. The emperor decreed an end to the games. Why? Because one man had the courage to say, "Enough is enough."

It's time to stir up the gift, to jump into the arena. It's time to demand a higher calling than playing games. The sides aren't balanced; we are outnumbered. When James Calvert went as a missionary to the cannibals in the Fiji Islands, the captain of the ship said, "You will lose your life and the lives of those with you if you go among such savages." Calvert replied, "We died before we came here."

We don't have time for average. Average is climbing halfway up the mountain and stopping. It's as close to great as it is to bad. It is a picture of a life that has lost zeal, passion, and fire. We hold a ReFRESH® conference twice a year. It's a call to spiritual awakening. In increasing numbers, younger pastors are coming. Our young people are coming in greater numbers than ever. Why? They want to give themselves to something greater.

We must call people to the fire. The coals have been cold for so long that it takes time to stoke them and fan the flame again. The altar of repentance is needed to burn away the dross that destroys the image of Christ in us.

Peter calls us to have a "sincere mind," a mind of purity. Plato used the word to refer to pure, uncontaminated reasoning. The Greek literally means "sun judged," as a piece of pottery was held up to the sun to see if there were any flaws or cracks in it. When the fire of God is stirred within us, we will allow ourselves to be examined by the Son.

What will happen if we don't call out this generation to stir up the fire and sell out to the Savior? The fire will go out. The church will be irrelevant. The blessings will be removed. Our families will be in bondage to the world, the flesh, and the devil.

I'm praying for God to give us a new generation of men like those who influenced my life. Men who never wavered from the Word. Men who stood courageously to call the church to repentance and holiness.

The Scriptures give us numerous admonitions to apply to our lives. Wake up (see 1 Thess. 5:1–11); clean up (see 1 John 2:28–3:3); grow up (see Rom. 13:14); stir up (see 2 Tim. 1:6). If the devil can't keep us from being saved, he will do the next best thing—he will make us content with average. He'll get us to leave the life of abandonment and accept the life of defeat.

What could happen if we took seriously the command to "keep ablaze the gift of God" and to invest in a Timothy? The church would grow by multiplication instead of addition. Within a few years, we would have a worldwide impact.

Let me set up a hypothetical situation for you. Let's suppose I was able to preach to 100,000 people every day, 365 days a year, and suppose that 4,000 came to Christ every day. At the end of one year, there would be 1,460,000 new believers. In just sixteen years, there would be 23,360,000. That would be impressive, wouldn't it?

Now let's suppose I used the principle of multiplication. Suppose I find a young Timothy, lead him to Christ, and pour into him for six months. Then I find another young man, and Timothy also finds another young man and begins to work with him. Every six months we (and they) lead someone else to Christ and mentor them. At the end of one year, we would have four, and at the end of two years, sixteen. At the end of sixteen years we would have four billion followers of Jesus Christ!

How is that possible? We take seriously the call to invest ourselves in others. We don't allow the fire to go out in our lives or theirs. We lead them to a point where they can lead others, and the process continues.

So get stirred up. Find your Timothy. Who will be first to answer that call?

Chapter 10

THE COURAGE TO FACE PERSECUTION

*"They were stoning Stephen as he called out: 'Lord
Jesus, receive my spirit!' Then he knelt down and
cried out with a loud voice, 'Lord, do not charge
them with this sin!' And saying this, he fell asleep."*
(Acts 7:59–60)

*"I'm accepting the fact that I need to learn
to do the hard things."*

—Adam Mitchell, *Courageous*

D o you know the name Richard Wurmbrand (1909–2001)?
He was a Jew who converted to Christianity in 1938
after studying Marxism in Moscow. In 1944, when
the Communists began to establish themselves in Romania,
Wurmbrand began a ministry that eventually went underground.
He was arrested on February 29, 1948, while on his way to
church. Over the next two decades he would be placed in
numerous penal facilities where he was tortured, spent three
years in solitary confinement, and was put to hard labor. After
eight and a half years in prison, Wurmbrand was released in

1956 and immediately went right back to his work in the underground church. Not long after, he was arrested and sentenced to twenty-five years, and he was again beaten and tortured severely.

Finally a release was negotiated, and Wurmbrand left the country. In 1966 he appeared before a Senate committee and took off his shirt in front of television cameras to reveal the scars of his torture. The following year he formed what would become The Voice of the Martyrs, an "inter-denominational Christian organization dedicated to assisting the persecuted church worldwide."

Some have said the persecuted church is the growing church. It seems to be true. While the church is exploding in Third World countries, the church is declining in America and Europe. Benjamin E. Fernando said, "Crushing the church is like smashing the atom: divine energy of high quality is released in enormous quantity with miraculous effects."

Billy Graham said, "It is unnatural for Christianity to be popular."[1] Maybe that's why the American church has become so insipid and apathetic. We cannot and should not expect better treatment than our Lord (see Matt. 10:17–20; John 15:18–19).

You can't read the book of Acts without coming face-to-face with the reality of persecution. Rather than causing the early church to crumble, it was the spark that ignited it. You would think it would be just the opposite. You would think the church would grow in times when it has materially prospered, but such is not the case. Persecution separates the wheat from the tares, the converted from the pretenders.

My friends Peter and Jetta Vidu serve the Second Baptist

Church of Oradea in Romania. I first met Peter a few years after the collapse of the Soviet Union, and he and his wife are two of the most godly, humble people I have ever met. They have been used mightily by God to build a phenomenal church in Oradea, complete with a school, a seminary, and a vibrant witness to the nation.

Under Communism, they lived with persecution and threats. Since the fall of Communism, there is a new persecution, which includes the Orthodox Church. In an interview in 1993, Peter said, "Always there has been persecution for the real Christians. And there are only two kinds of persecution: pagan persecution and religious persecution. We have had a pagan persecution under the Communists, and now we are threatened with a religious persecution."

Persecution is a reality for believers around the world. Christians are becoming the targets of governments and other religions. The Voice of the Martyrs blog notes:

> The persecution facing Christians is the largest "human rights" violation issue in today's world. However, it is impossible to know with absolute certainty the exact number of Christians who are killed each year for their faith.
>
> According to the World Evangelical Alliance, over 200 million Christians in at least 60 countries are denied fundamental human rights solely because of their faith. David B. Barrett, Todd M. Johnson, and Peter F. Crossing in their 2009 report in the International Bulletin of Missionary Research (Vol. 33, No. 1: 32) estimate that approximately 176,000 Christians will

have been martyred from mid-2008 to mid-2009. This, according to the authors, compares to 160,000 martyrs in mid-2000 and 34,400 at the beginning of the 20th century. If current trends continue, Barrett, Johnson and Crossing estimate that by 2025, an average of 210,000 Christians will be martyred annually (http://persecutedchurch.blogspot.com).

Although it is hard for us to imagine this, it seems the pattern is following similar lines as those used by the Germans against the Jews in the 1930s and 1940s. It is a strategy of slowly isolating and discriminating. You don't have to look far to realize there are those in our land who are seeking to marginalize the church and believers. Once you instill racism or prejudice against a people—whether on the basis of race, creed, or religion—you can begin to ramp up the establishment of laws hindering those groups and ultimately justify persecuting them. It was simple at first—just take prayer, the Bible, and the Ten Commandments out of our public institutions. Make it difficult for cities and communities to display anything religious on public property. Once you've established a pattern, the generations that follow eventually know nothing of our nation's religious heritage.

A few years ago a woman in Houston, Texas, was told she could not hand out gospel tracts to kids knocking on her door during Halloween. In another state an organization hands out material to schoolchildren entitled, "We Can Be Good without God." All of this was reinforced to me when I recently read S. E. Cupp's book, *Losing Our Religion*. Though an atheist, Cupp recognizes the liberal media's attacks on Christianity and writes of their long-term effects on our land.

We may not live to see the days when we face severe persecution, but on whatever level opposition comes, we are called to be faithful and courageous. If our passion is to please God and to give Him glory, we will face growing persecution. In light of that, on a scale of one to ten, how would you rate your passion to advance the glory of God? Are you in any way ashamed of identifying yourself as a believer in Christ?

As you read Acts, you are introduced to Stephen. He was one of the first deacons and was the first martyr of the church in Jerusalem. He was a man who knew how to live and was prepared to die (see Acts 6:5, 8; 7:55).

When the persecution of the church was in its earliest stages, Stephen, along with the disciples, was a key spokesperson. He has to be counted among one of the great men of the Bible as he helped set the tone for the early church. It is no exaggeration to say that his martyrdom was a "pivotal and epoch-making moment in the ongoing purpose of God. . . . Everything in the first half of the book of Acts leads up to it and stems from it."[2]

Vance Havner said, "There are not two gospels, one for missionaries and martyrs, the other for those who name the name of Christ but let Him bear the Cross alone while they themselves go free." On the heels of the outpouring of the Spirit, there was growing resentment and persecution of the church by the religious leaders. They saw Christ as a threat to their way of life. In the face of growing opposition, Stephen stood up to defend the faith.

Stephen's defense of the faith brought about such anger and opposition that the religious leaders were enraged by him.

Stephen was persecuted and eventually stoned to death as the first martyr. The word *martyr* means witness, one who gives testimony. With the death of Stephen, the term took on new meaning as one who would die for the faith.

Stephen was not a seminary graduate. He wasn't even a mature believer and had probably been saved less than five years. Yet he gave himself totally to Christ and displayed a maturity and boldness rarely seen in the local church today. Stephen was full of God. The Holy Spirit empowered him to live an extraordinary life even in the face of derision and death. Stephen loved God, and God delighted in putting him in a position where He could shine.

It would be hard to examine the short life of Stephen and not come to the conclusion, "This is a man!" When brought before the religious leaders, Stephen did not tremble in fear. Although they saw Stephen as a problem, he saw them as an opportunity to preach Christ. It drove them crazy (see Acts 6:9–14).

What made Stephen a courageous man? He was full of the Spirit. "Therefore, brothers, select from among you seven men of good reputation, full of the Spirit and wisdom" (Acts 6:3). If we are going to have courageous leaders in the church, we can't underestimate the importance of those three characteristics. Not just for deacons but for anyone who is serious about the things of God.

God's design is for us to walk in the fullness of the Spirit. It is a command for us to be "filled by the Spirit" (Eph. 5:18). It is impossible to be courageous in the faith without the filling of the Spirit. Stephen lived in the overflow of the Spirit. The difference between the first-century church and the twenty-first-century church is that they were power conscious and we are problem conscious. They weren't perfect, but they had a standard that we too often compromise because of fear.

Stephen was also full of wisdom, faith, and power, able to make decisions and choices controlled by the Spirit. He was wise enough to know he needed God's wisdom. He didn't run ahead of God or act on his own (1 Cor. 6:19–20). Stephen could cut to the chase and see the real issues behind the facades. In fact, Luke wrote, "they were unable to stand up against his wisdom and the Spirit by whom he [Stephen] was speaking" (Acts 6:10).

Acts 7 is the record of his sermon and response to the religious leaders. It is the longest sermon in the book of Acts, but Stephen didn't waste time addressing the false charges. He was single-minded, focused on the story of God's plan of redemption. Why was this significant? Because it reveals a man whose mind was saturated with the Word of God. He knew his Bible. He knew the people, the history, and the purpose of it all. The Holy Spirit took what he knew and empowered him to communicate it clearly, concisely, and without apology.

Today Americans are biblically illiterate. We know little of the precious promises and unchanging commands of the Word of God. A. W. Pink said, "No verse of Scripture yields its meaning to lazy people."[3] You can't defend what you don't know. The great R. A. Torrey wrote, "Ninety-nine Christians in every hundred are merely playing at Bible study, and therefore ninety-nine Christians in every hundred are merely weaklings when they might be giants."[4] If you just know a little here and there, you'll come to the wrong conclusions.

Stephen was a man who knew the Scriptures. He didn't just have them in his head; he hid them in his heart. He was a student of the stories of God's faithfulness. Unfortunately some people know just enough to be dangerous. I would encourage you: make sure you are sitting under the preaching of a man of God who accurately handles the Word of God.

We need believers who know what they believe and why they believe it. We need Christ followers who will not waver or follow strange doctrines. If you don't know what you believe, you will never be able to figure out where you should stand. One thing you can know for certain is that the Holy Spirit will never lead you to do anything inconsistent with the life of Christ or the revealed Word of God.

Stephen was a man full of faith. His faith gave him courage to face opposition and believe God for the strength to stand against it. When you read Hebrews 11, the great faith chapter, you discover that people of faith always *did* something. Faith is active, not passive. Faith is confident that God will do what He says. Faith follows God implicitly.

Faith looks to God; it doesn't trust in itself or in personal abilities or strength. Faith takes God at His Word and obeys without hesitation or reservation. Someone has said it well, "Faith has no back door." Faith never panics. Rather, it leads us to claim a promise, take a stand, accept a difficult assignment, or surrender to go to a far-off land. Whereas Thomas was full of doubt, Stephen was full of faith.

Stephen was also full of grace, as his countenance revealed. "And all who were sitting in the Sanhedrin looked intently at him and saw that his face was like the face of an angel" (Acts 6:15). The peace of God was present on his face even in the face of persecution. I've seen panic on the faces of believers at red lights, in traffic jams, and amid the simplest setbacks. These seventy Jewish leaders were doing all they could to attack Stephen, but he seemed unaffected by it all. His countenance radiated with the grace of Jesus. Even in the face of his accusers, he was gracious in offering them an opportunity to come to Christ. One writer said, "It challenged his foes and charmed his friends." His life overflowed with the grace of God.

God's grace makes us like Jesus. God's grace gave Stephen what he needed to be a witness, whether to a widow or to someone who wanted to war with him. God's grace through Stephen was amazing and abounding. And that same grace is sufficient anywhere we go, anytime we need it. As someone has said, "The will of God will never lead you where the grace of God cannot keep you."

Stephen was a man full of power, not according to the world's ideals but to God's. The thirst for power drives this world. It drives dictators, Wall Street, and Washington. But ultimately, all the powers of this world will come to an end. Stephen's power did not come through a position or title; it came from the Holy Spirit. His was not the power of a magnetic personality. Rather, it was the personality of the person of the Holy Spirit that shone through all Stephen did and said. The Holy Spirit enabled him to "proclaim the gospel, defend the faith, and endure a martyr's death."[5]

While we live in a power-hungry, power-conscious world, we should learn the difference between temporary power and God's abiding power. We serve the God with power to create, redeem, sustain, and overrule. We need power for living. Our lives should reveal the Spirit's empowerment to live as Christ intends for us to live. Remember, the promise of the Spirit's coming was accompanied by the promise of His power (see Acts 1:8). If you are going to be courageous, you need power.

> And the apostles were giving testimony with great power to the resurrection of the Lord Jesus, and great grace was on all of them. (Acts 4:33)

> For I am not ashamed of the gospel, because it is God's power for salvation to everyone who believes, first to the Jew, and also to the Greek. (Rom. 1:16)

> My speech and my proclamation were not with persuasive words of wisdom but with a powerful demonstration by the Spirit, so that your faith might not be based on men's wisdom but on God's power. (1 Cor. 2:4–5)

Stephen, full of the Spirit, had power to preach and power to face the persecution. He had power to stand and power to suffer. He was able to exalt Christ and endure for Christ. This resulted in his ability even to pray for his persecutors.

Where are the lives that exemplify courageous power today? Where are the men and women who have a holy boldness? God gave Stephen power to proclaim the truth in the face of a hostile crowd.

> You stiff-necked people with uncircumcised hearts and ears! You are always resisting the Holy Spirit; as

your ancestors did, so do you. Which of the prophets did your fathers not persecute? They even killed
those who announced beforehand the coming of the
Righteous One, whose betrayers and murderers you
have now become. (Acts 7:51–52)

A man full of power not only knows how to act, but he
also knows how to react. However, Stephen's opponents didn't
react kindly.

When they heard these things, they were enraged
in their hearts and gnashed their teeth at him. But
Stephen, filled by the Holy Spirit, gazed into heaven.
He saw God's glory, with Jesus standing at the right
hand of God, and he said, "Look! I see the heavens
opened and the Son of Man standing at the right
hand of God!" Then they screamed at the top of their
voices, covered their ears, and together rushed against
him. They threw him out of the city and began to
stone him. And the witnesses laid their robes at the
feet of a young man named Saul. They were stoning Stephen as he called out: "Lord Jesus, receive my
spirit!" Then he knelt down and cried out with a loud
voice, "Lord, do not charge them with this sin!" And
saying this, he fell asleep. (Acts 7:54–60)

Even as he was being stoned, Stephen made the same two
requests Jesus made at the cross: receive my spirit and forgive
them. We know at least two who heard his cries that day—
Saul, who would later give his life to follow Christ; and Jesus,

who stood at the right hand of God. Think about it, the last person Stephen talked to on earth was Jesus, and the first person he saw in heaven was Jesus. Quite an exit, wouldn't you say?

The American church is not ready for persecution. We aren't the stuff of which martyrs are made. We are wimpy, self-serving, and self-centered, dining on pabulum and watered-down Christianity. One of my favorite illustrations ever used by Ron Dunn was entitled "Braving the Rain." He wrote the following article for his church newsletter at MacArthur Boulevard Baptist Church after reading another pastor's article thanking his members for "braving the rain" to come to church.

> I want to thank all of you who BRAVED THE RAIN last Sunday morning to attend church. Such sacrifice and suffering humbled me. I can imagine how it must be to awaken to the petrifying noise of rain. Dedication hangs in the balance. The silky voice of the Tempter whispers in your ear: "Don't be foolish! Why risk your life?"
>
> Suddenly, your shoulders snap to attention, the jaw sets in determination. "Get thee behind me, Satan!" you shout, "and hang the crease in my pants." Then, counting not your life dear unto yourself and side-stepping treacherous mud holes, you splash through the deluge to your waiting car.
>
> Demonstrating raw courage, you navigate your four-wheeled ark over three blocks of slippery streets, while the rain slams against your windshield like silver bullets. Surely, this deserves a place among those other

heroic exploits of the faithful: "they were stoned, they were sawn asunder, were tempted, were slain with the sword; they wandered about in sheepskins and goatskins; being destitute, afflicted, tortured, THEY BRAVED THE RAIN."

Reaching the church, you once again take your life into your hands and with nerves of steel, plunge from the drenched car and over soppy sidewalks to the dry haven of the classroom.

As I stand at my window watching this spectacle, my heart swells. I hear distant applause—strange applause—wings clapping?

I can hardly preach. I feel I must write a new edition of *Foxes Book of Christian Martyrs*. How the world must have gasped in unbelief and admiration as they saw you BRAVE THE RAIN.

The cross demands more of us! The twenty-first century finds us facing increased persecution in America. We can no longer expect (and maybe we don't deserve) preferential treatment. In a generation absorbed with celebrities, we need stand-up men like Stephen.

I've stood at the gate where Stephen was stoned to death two thousand years ago and wondered, where are the young men who will stand at the gates of our cities and call the people back to God? We need boldness in this land of the bland. We need passion in the midst of apathy. We need a Stephen, "full of the Spirit and wisdom" (Acts 6:3). Will you be the one to answer that call? When all around you may be falling, can God trust you to stand?

HE'S MY INSPIRATION

I've written about several of my favorite Bible characters in this book. Dozens of other examples are found in the Scriptures. The one I find myself most attracted to is our Lord Jesus. He inspires me to courageously face legalism and dead religion. He empowers me to be courageous. He gives me courage instead of fear. He has defeated everything I could ever be afraid of. Hebrews 12:1–3 says,

> Therefore, since we also have such a large cloud of witnesses surrounding us, let us lay aside every weight and the sin that so easily ensnares us. Let us run with endurance the race that lies before us, keeping our eyes on Jesus, the source and perfecter of our faith, who for the joy that lay before Him endured a cross and despised the shame and has sat down at the right hand of God's throne. For consider Him who endured such hostility from sinners against Himself, so that you won't grow weary and lose heart.

Jesus would not turn away from Gethsemane or the cross. At every point Jesus pleased His heavenly Father. Warren Wiersbe notes, "Jesus lived and ministered on earth in the power of the Spirit (Acts 10:37–38), and so must we. It is unfortunate that so many believers think that Jesus served as He did simply because He was God and exercised His divine powers. They argue that because they don't have the same divine nature as Jesus, God can't expect too much from them; but this kind of thinking is all wrong. When He served here on earth, Jesus depended on the Holy Spirit, prayer and the Word of God, and these divine resources are available to us today."[1]

Far too many believers fall short of God's expectations. Fear, cowardice, baggage from the past, and a thousand other things cripple us. Instead of walking in victory, we just limp along and get along. The landscape of the Old Testament is littered with the bodies of God's people, long forgotten, who died in the wilderness because of their unbelief and lack of courage. The history of the twenty-first-century American church may be the story of masses of church members who lived insipid, uninspiring lives and settled for less than God's best.

Unfortunately the majority of God's people live something less than courageous lives. They are marked by defeat more than victory, fear more than faith, timidity more than boldness. Why? The sin of settling. Settling for second best. Settling for what is comfortable. Settling for less than God designed us to be. It's not enough to be good enough.

We find the command to "be strong and courageous" twenty-six times in the Old Testament. Three times we see the phrase, "Be strong and let your heart take courage." We obviously identify those words with Joshua. This great leader is my Old Testament hero. His name means "Jehovah saves."

Joshua was a courageous soldier, father, and leader who called those around him to be courageous. His courage came because he was faithful. Unlike the majority of his peers, he never backed down from a battle or stopped believing God for the land.

This is no time to stand still or hesitate when there is so much to be done. We will find courage in the Word of God and the will of God. Living the courageous life is being willing to pray, "Not my will but God's be done."

We are in a battle. Battles require preparation. For the believer, prep time is spent in the Word and in prayer. Joshua was told to meditate on the Word. The fact that Jesus spent time alone in prayer reminds me there is no power to face the battles of life without the Word and prayer. Alan Redpath wrote that a person God uses has to "know what it is to pay the price of a closed door." Jesus was a person of prayer and a student of His own Word. He would go off alone to pray because He knew "the price of a closed door." If God in the flesh needed time to communicate with God the Father, can we do any less?

Jesus quoted the Scriptures in a variety of settings. He reminded the Pharisees of what God had said when they tried to twist the Scriptures for their benefit. He cleaned out the temple so it could be a house of prayer. The Word is "living and effective and sharper than any double-edged sword" (Heb. 4:12), and all the promises of God find their yes in Christ (see 2 Cor. 1:20).

If you want to find courage, get on your knees and get in the Word. The pages of Scripture are filled with the life stories of His champions. They weren't famous because they were talented or gifted but because they had the courage to stand. They never quit. Patriarchs, prophets, and first-century preachers all drew courage from an intimate relationship with the living God. They wouldn't bow or bend to anyone but God and God alone.

Every page and every story drives me to Jesus. He is the greatest game changer, difference maker, and influencer in human history. Philip Schaff points out, "Jesus of Nazareth, without money and arms, conquered more millions than Alexander, Caesar, Mohammed, and Napoleon; without science and learning, He shed more light on things human and divine than all philosophers and scholars combined; without the eloquence of schools, He spoke such words of life as were never spoken before or since and produces effects which lie beyond the reach of orator or poet; without writing a single line, He set more pens in motion, and furnished themes for more sermons, orations, discussions, learned volumes, works of art, and songs of praise than the whole army of great men of ancient and modern times."[2]

Jesus faced critics, cynics, and skeptics and never blinked. He faced the devil in the wilderness and never backed down from the Word. He faced the cross and never looked back. He was born to die. He chose the hour and place of His coming at Bethlehem. He chose the time and place of His death at Golgatha on an old rugged cross. From birth until death, the Son of Man had total control of His life. Men did not take His life; He gave it freely. When His body was laid in a borrowed tomb, it looked as if the devil had won. It appeared that mortal men like Herod, Caiaphas, and Pilate had stopped Him. But three days later Jesus stepped out of the tomb. He won the day. That resurrection power is ours today. The challenge is to apply it on a daily basis, not just to sing about it at church.

We live in difficult times. Our brothers and sisters around the world are being persecuted for their faith. In many lands becoming a Christian is a literal death sentence. This world is not evolving into something better. It is becoming more and more like the days of the Roman Empire when Christians were tortured and persecuted for believing in Jesus as the Son of God. This is no time for cowards. We need a courageous leader. Will you be the one? Will you stand, even if you have to stand alone? Will you find yourself in the company of men like those we've examined in these pages, or will you be another forgotten life buried in a graveyard of mediocrity?

In AD 168 an old bishop named Polycarp was led before an angry crowd to be killed for his faith. As the bishop of Smyrna, he was the last living link to the original disciples, having studied under the apostle John. The Roman government tried to get Polycarp to deny Christ. He said, "Eighty-six years I have served the Lord Jesus Christ, and He never once wronged me. How can I blaspheme my King who has saved me?"

At that point the Roman proconsul threatened to throw Polycarp to the wild beasts or burn him at the stake. He courageously responded, "You threaten me with fire which will burn for an hour and then will go out, but you are ignorant of the fire of the future judgment of God reserved for the everlasting torment of the ungodly. But why do you delay? Bring on the beasts, or the fire, or whatever you choose; you shall not move me to deny Christ, my Lord and Savior."[3]

In his final prayer Polycarp prayed, "O Father, I thank You that You have called me to this day and hour and have counted me worthy to receive my place along with the number of the holy martyrs."[4]

God's Word, God's Son, and His indwelling Spirit empower us to be courageous. We have nothing to fear in this life or in death.

NOTES

Introduction

1. Andrew Romano and Tony Dokopil, "Man Up! The Traditional Male Is an Endangered Species," *Time* magazine (September 27, 2010).

2. Ibid.

Chapter 1

1. John Blanchard, *The Complete Gathered Gold: A Treasury of Quotations for Christians* (Evangelical Press, 2006), 296.

2. Warren Wiersbe, *Life Sentences* (Grand Rapids: Zondervan, 2007), 43.

3. James Montgomery Boice, *Genesis Volume 2: A New Beginning (Genesis 12–36)* (Baker Book House), accessed via WORDsearch.

Chapter 2

1. John Mason, *Know Your Limits—Then Ignore Them* (Tulsa: Insight Publishing Group, 1999), 125.

2. Vance Havner, *Moments of Decision* (Fleming H. Revell, 1979).

3. Mrs. Howard Taylor, *Borden of Yale '09* (Philadelphia: China Inland Mission, 1926), 75.

4. Ibid., ix.

5. Vance Havner, *Moments of Decision*.

6. Donald Whitney, *Spiritual Disciplines for the Christian Life* (NavPress, 1997), 187.

Chapter 3

1. Lloyd John Ogilvie, *Lord of the Impossible* (Nashville: Abingdon, 1984), 99.

2. C. H. Spurgeon, *Sermons on Men of the Old Testament* (Grand Rapids: Zondervan), 131.

3. Roy Laurin, *Meet Yourself in the Bible* (Chicago: Moody Press, 1970), 79.

Chapter 4

1. "A Person on Purpose" (Keswick, Cumbria, England: Keswick Ministries and Authentic Media, 2005), 109.

2. Gary Inrig, *Hearts of Iron Feet of Clay* (Grand Rapids: Discovery House Publishers, 2005), 90.

3. Warren Wiersbe, *Life Sentences* (Grand Rapids: Zondervan, 2007), 109.

4. Gary Inrig, *Hearts of Iron Feet of Clay*, 100.

5. Roy B. Zuck, *The Speaker's Quote Book: Over 5,000 Illustrations and Quotations for All Occasions* (Kregel, 2009).

6. Ron Dunn, *The Faith Crisis* (Tyndale House, 1984), 69–70.

Chapter 5

1. Warren Wiersbe, *Put Your Life Together: Studies in the Book of Ruth* (Lincoln, NE: Back to the Bible Publications, 1985), 74..

2. *Dictionary of Biblical Imagery* (InterVarsity Christian Fellowship, 1998), accessed via WORDsearch.

3. Warren Wiersbe, *Put Your Life Together*.

4. This story has been adapted and summarized from an article in *Missions Mosaic*, November 2003, by Jeanie Mclean and from a BP article by Jami Becher.

Chapter 6

1. Thom S. Rainer and Jess Rainer, *The Millennials* (Nashville: B&H Publishing Group, 2011).

2. Alex and Brett Harris, *Do Hard Things* (Colorado Springs: Multnomah, 2008), 29–30.

3. John Blanchard, *The Complete Gathered Gold: A Treasury of Quotations for Christians* (Evangelical Press, 2006), 673.

4. Vance Harner, *On This Rock I Stand* (Grand Rapids: Baker, 1981), 66.

5. *Reader's Digest*, July 1964.

6. *The New Rebellion Handbook* (Nashville: Thomas Nelson, 2006), 254–60.

Chapter 7

1. Vance Havner, *Moments of Decision* (Grand Rapids: Fleming H. Revell, 1979).
2. C. H. Spurgeon, *Metropolitan Tabernacle Pulpit: 0800–0899*, "0856—The Importunate Widow," accessed via WORDSearch.
3. Vance Havner, *Moments of Decision*, 68–69.

Chapter 8

1. "Citizenship in a Republic," speech at Sorbonne, Paris, April 23, 1910.
2. Cyril Barber, *Nehemiah and the Dynamics of Effective Leadership* (Neptune, NJ: Loizeaux Brothers, 1991), 65.
3. Charles Swindoll, *Hand Me Another Brick* (Nashville: Thomas Nelson, 1998), 67.
4. Roy Laurin, *Meet Yourself in the Bible* (Chicago: Kampen Press, 1946), 120.

Chapter 10

1. John Blanchard, *The Complete Gathered Gold: A Treasury of Quotations for Christians* (Evangelical Press, 2006), 76.
2. J. Oswald Sanders, *People Just Like Us* (Chicago: Moody Press, 1978), 177–78.
3. John Blanchard, *The Complete Gathered Gold: A Treasury of Quotations for Christians*, 61.
4. Ibid., 63.
5. J. Oswald Sanders, *People Just Like Us*, 181.

Epilogue

1. Warren Wiersbe, *Life Sentences* (Grand Rapids: Zondervan, 2007), 221.
2. Philip Schaff, *The Person of Christ* (New York: American Tract Society, 1913), 33.
3. Quoted *Jesus Freaks*, (Bethany House Publishers, 1999), 136.
4. Ibid.

Leading your family
takes courage.

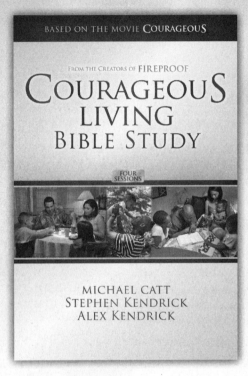

COURAGEOUS LIVING
Bible Study Curriculum Kit

This dynamic four-week study facilitates leading men toward living more courageously in four key areas:

Responsibility: serving, protecting, and casting a vision for their family
Priorities: focusing on eternal things rather than what is temporary
Legacy: emphasizing a father's potential impact as a godly role model
Faith: strengthening a father's identity in Christ

Kit includes one 64-page member book and a DVD-ROM featuring *Courageous* film clips to support each lesson.

Also Available
Courageous Living
Bible Study Member Book

IAmCourageous.com

FROM THE CREATORS OF
FIREPROOF

COURAGEOUS
HONOR BEGINS AT HOME

Four men, one calling: To serve and protect. When tragedy strikes home, these men are left wrestling with their hopes, their fears, their faith, and their fathering. Protecting the streets is second nature. Raising their children in a God-honoring way? That's courageous.

"But as for me and my household, we will serve the Lord." Joshua 24:15

COURAGEOUSTHEMOVIE.COM

facebook.
courageousthemovie

twitter
@courageousmovie

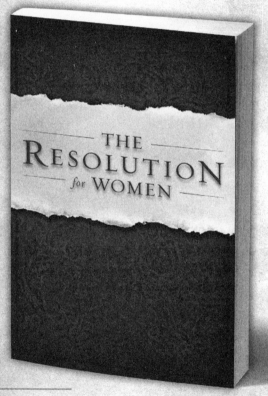

Do You Have the Courage to Do the Courageous Bible Study?

First you have to commit to the full eight weeks. Then you need the resilience to stick it out once God begins to reveal your weak spots. Then you need the guts to work through those shortcomings. And we're not just talking about the men. Women also have a role to play, and it may be much different than what you're doing now.

We fully expect that some people won't have the courage to do this study. We also expect that those who do will be changed forever, along with their family and their church. Find out more about *Honor Begins at Home: The Courageous Bible Study* at www.IAmCourageous.com, 800.458.2772, or the LifeWay Christian Store serving you.

www.IAmCourageous.com

LifeWay | Adults

BREAKING
THROUGH

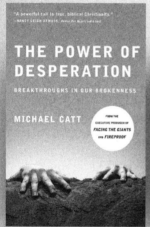

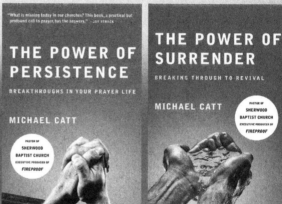

"A powerful call to true, biblical Christianity."
—NANCY LEIGH DEMOSS, *Revive Our Hearts radio host*

THE POWER OF DESPERATION
BREAKTHROUGHS IN OUR BROKENNESS

MICHAEL CATT

FROM THE
EXECUTIVE PRODUCER OF
FACING THE GIANTS
AND *FIREPROOF*

"What is missing today in our churches? This book, a practical but profound call to prayer, has the answers." —JAY STRACK

THE POWER OF PERSISTENCE
BREAKTHROUGHS IN YOUR PRAYER LIFE

MICHAEL CATT

PASTOR OF
SHERWOOD
BAPTIST CHURCH
EXECUTIVE PRODUCER OF
FIREPROOF

THE POWER OF SURRENDER
BREAKING THROUGH TO REVIVAL

MICHAEL CATT

PASTOR OF
SHERWOOD
BAPTIST CHURCH
EXECUTIVE PRODUCER OF
FIREPROOF

THE ReFRESH SERIES

Michael Catt, senior pastor of Sherwood Baptist Church and executive producer of the Georgia congregation's popular films *Flywheel, Facing the Giants, Fireproof,* and *Courageous*, examines brokenness, prayer, and revival in his ReFresh series.

BHPublishingGroup.com

ReFRESH®

A Conference for those who thirst for Revival...

ReFRESH® is a conference founded by Pastor Michael Catt for those who thirst for revival. It's not about church growth or the latest worship fads. It's a time for you to come apart from the distractions and chaos of life and seek the face of God. We invite you to join us at Sherwood Baptist Church every September for ReFRESH® or in the beauty of the Smoky Mountains every spring for ReFRESH® in the Smokies, and experience times of refreshing in the presence of the Lord. There are plenty of conferences and events out there, but this one is different.

This one is uplifting... transformational... ReFRESHing.

For more information on ReFRESH® and ReFRESH® in the Smokies, visit

WWW.REFRESHCONFERENCE.ORG

PREPARE FOR RAIN
The Story of a Church that Believed God for the Impossible

Follow the story of Pastor Michael Catt and his congregation as the Lord changes a "typical Southern Baptist church" into a ministry center that reaches thousands and has even challenged the Hollywood establishment with their locally produced, nationally syndicated movies.

AVAILABLE IN STORES AND ONLINE
AT WWW.SHERWOODBAPTIST.NET

FIREPROOF YOUR LIFE
Building a Faith that Survives the Flames

Using illustrations from his own life and from the movie, *Fireproof*, Catt discusses practical issues such as temptation, marriage and finances, helping us build a faith that resists our corrosive culture. Rather than succumb to the pressure of circumstances, we can stand tall and face our challenges in Christ's power.

AVAILABLE IN STORES AND ONLINE
AT WWW.SHERWOODBAPTIST.NET

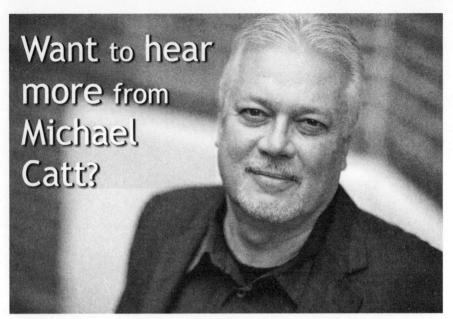